India @ _ _

Reflections on New India

India @ 75

Reflections on New India

Editor

Nivedita Das Kundu

Vij Books
New Delhi (India)

Published by

Vij Books
(Publishers, Distributors & Importers)
4836/24, Ansari Road
Delhi – 110 002
Phones: 91-11-43596460
M: 98110 94883
E-mail: contact@vijpublishing.com
Web : www.vijbooks.in

ISBN: 978-81-19438-95-2 (Paperback)

Dedicated to

Students of International Relations

Contents

Preface

This Book is the outcome of research conducted by senior scholars from Bharat Centre of Canada (BCC), United Service Institution of India (USI), Manohar Parrikar Institute for Defence Studies and Analyses (MPIDSA), Security Risks Asia, Maulana Azad National Urdu University (MANUU) and Institution of Eminence, University of Delhi.

When Narendra Modi led *Bharatiya Janata Party* (BJP) came to power in 2014, it was for the first time that a political party had secured absolute majority in Lok Sabha, lower house of India's parliament. He was able to repeat his performance and secured a second term in 2019 in an election in which India's security and foreign policy played an important role. There has been a keen interest to analyse PM Modi's policies not only in India but in other nations as well. This edited volume aims to bring out key elements of PM Modi's policies during his second term, also called Modi 2.0, in critical areas that are important for India's national security, science and technology, defence reforms, Indo-Pacific, China challenge in South Asia, on Tibet issue, Northeast India and Andaman and Nicobar Islands. A key idea that has emerged from this volume is that at a time when global politics has become further complex and uncertain due to Russia-Ukraine crisis and the negative economic impact due to COVID-19 pandemic, a strong and stable leadership in India was able to take decisive actions to navigate India through these testing times. It is already visible as India has convinced the Western nations about its national security imperatives being the prime factors behind India's continued engagement with Russia. Even in India, the diplomatic stand taken by the Modi administration has been approved by all the opposition parties. One of the key lessons that India has learnt from the Russia-Ukraine crisis is that India has to be self-dependent (*Atmanirbhar*) in areas like defence. *Atmanirbhar Bharat* ISelf dependent India) is already a flagship campaign of Modi government and in coming years, this trend is likely to intensify. India would not aspire for the status of a balancing power but to be a leading power. India aims to be an independent pole in the global order, allowing New Delhi to emerge as a rule shaper. These efforts are at the centre of policies being implemented by Modi 2.0.

In the field of science and technology and military modernisation, India would look to carve its own space for its technology requirements. What India demands more than ever, and the strategies the incumbent Modi government should focus on would be to find a stable and competent partner in ICT (Information and Communication Technology) and outer space. It is essential not to get pulled into the scuffle between the great powers but rather keep India's interests in mind and focus on leveraging better opportunities afforded by the tech-hungry country like India. There is a major need for the government to ensure significant growth in foreign investments in various technological sectors. Also, there is a need to engage Indian diaspora very effectively at various levels. They can contribute both in terms of investments and expertise.

In the recent years, the government of India has undertaken some path breaking decisions in terms of demonstration of hard power such as the surgical strikes and the *Shakti* -Anti-Satellite tests. On defense reform in terms of strategy that PM Modi can be credited with is in bringing in an offensive strategy in dealing with state sponsored acts of terrorism (surgical strikes). Although it has been claimed that such actions were taken by earlier governments also, the difference is that they were surprise, covert & undeclared, controlled retaliation. In current case, the strikes are overt, declared and the risk of escalation is higher. PM Modi took the decisive step of taking this risk. The Modi era will be remembered as one where for the first time Pakistan's nuclear no-nonsense was called off and escalation control was kept with India. India's defense policy while pursuing a combination of proactive and reactive aggression is likely to focus on medium to long term capability building to strengthen deterrence. Towards this end, innovative funding, prioritising, restructuring and self-reliance will be main way ahead. India needs a technology ecosystem suited to Indian conditions supported by all the stakeholders, not the military alone. The other stakeholders would include the academia, universities and the private sector. Make-in-India needs technology push while investments are needed in military start ups like in case of Israel. Defence start ups need greater hand holding by the government and the private sector to modernise Indian military.

PM Modi has undertaken some fundamental changes in India's internal security management by abrogating Article 370 in Jammu & Kashmir while economic, political and security situation is being improved in the north eastern states of India as part of India's Act East policy. Reorganisation of J&K would allow the Central government to sideline vested interests and deliver good governance to people. This is needed to delegitimise the radical elements as they would lose their support since the social contract between the government and the people in the region would be strengthened. The battle of narrative will be spearheaded by the people, battle of guns by the security forces and healing touch by the government. Government of India is also working to ensure economic interdependence between India's north eastern states and the countries in Southeast Asia as part of Act East policy. Another important aspect pertains to the strategic location of Andaman and Nicobar islands; a geographical asset for India in the Indo-Pacific. Development of these islands, both in economic and security terms fits in India's Act East and Indo Pacific policies. The economic element of Indo Pacific strategy is weak and India would need to make efforts to strengthen the trade aspects with like-minded countries like the United States of America , Japan, Australia and South Korea. Expanding the economic agenda under the QUAD countries could potentially begin to strengthen the geo-economic aspects in the Indo-Pacific.

One of the main purposes of this book is to familiarise the readers, academics and students of international relations, about the New India. The Bharat Centre of Canada is already doing a lot of work. This book further intensifies these efforts through contributions from think tank and university experts from premier institutions in India. This Book is expected to fill in the existing gap in the literature on above-mentioned subjects and provide valuable inputs to policy planners in this regard.

Nivedita Das Kundu

Acknowledgements

The creation of this book, "India@75: Reflection on New India," emerged from a dedicated effort to foster deeper insights into the subject. The existence of this book owes itself to the unwavering backing and encouragement extended by academics, scholars, strategic analysts, foreign policy experts, practitioners, and policymakers. Their valuable insights and contributions have illuminated various pertinent topics, forming the cornerstone of this endeavour.

A debt of gratitude is owed to my colleagues and friends within the strategic community for their invaluable support. Their tireless dedication and contributions amidst their busy schedules have been instrumental in shaping this compiled volume. I must emphasize that without their steadfast support, this undertaking would not have come to existence. Special mention goes to Dr. Raj Kumar and Group Captain Sharad Tiwari, who provided indispensable inputs by meticulously reviewing the manuscript. Their support has been truly exceptional.

A heartfelt acknowledgment is extended to all the contributors, whose collaborative spirit and willingness to share their profound knowledge have enriched this work. Their insightful and thought-provoking ideas have infused this book with depth and significance.

I am also indebted to my family members, whose unwavering support and cooperative attitude have been a pillar of strength throughout this research project's execution and the subsequent completion of this edited volume. Their contribution cannot be adequately expressed in words, and their presence has been invaluable.

Furthermore, I would like to extend my gratitude to the administrative and academic teams, students, and volunteers of the Bharat Centre of Canada. Their encouragement and cooperation have played a pivotal role in this endeavour. I would also like to thank the libraries of United Services Institution of India, Brampton City Library, and York University Library for their unwavering support, even though space constraints prevent me from acknowledging them individually. Their contributions have been deeply appreciated.

In its current form, this volume stands as a testament to the wholehearted collaboration and assistance of all the contributors. It is my sincere hope that readers, students of International Relations, foreign policy analysts, and policymakers will find value in the chapters of "India@75: Reflection on New India."

Nivedita Das Kundu

Editor & Contributors

Dr. Nivedita Das Kundu

Dr. Nivedita Das Kundu,(Ph.D) is a distinguished academic with extensive experience in university teaching and think tank research, specializing in International Relations. She is affiliated with the York University in Toronto and Alatoo-International University, Bishkek, where she holds Associate Professors position in International Relations. She is presently teaching Bachelor's and Master's students and supervising Ph.D students at a State University in Tashkent under Ministry of Higher Education, Science and Innovation of Republic of Uzbekistan, as an Associate Professor of International Relations.

Dr. Nivedita's educational background includes a Master's and doctoral studies from Jawaharlal Nehru University, New Delhi, and the University of Helsinki, Finland. She further pursued post-doctoral studies at the Woodrow Wilson Centre for Scholars in Washington DC. Throughout her career, she has contributed to academia and research by teaching at renowned institutions across the globe, including universities in Canada, Germany, Finland, India, Kyrgyzstan, Kazakhstan, Russia, China and Azerbaijan. Her expertise has been sought after by prestigious government think tanks such as the Institute for Defence Studies and Analyses, Indian Council for World Affairs, Indian Council for Social Science Research, United Services Institution of India, and the Centre for Strategic Studies under the President of Azerbaijan.

Dr. Nivedita's international engagement is evident through her roles as a visiting fellow at institutions like Moscow State Institute for International Relations, Moscow State University, Institute for Oriental Studies in Russia, Institute for International Relations in Kiev, and the School of International Relations at Sichuan University, Center for Russia, East European and Eurasian studies, University of Texas and at St Edward University. She is a prolific author, having authored two books and edited seven others on subjects related to International Relations. Her research contributions encompass research papers, articles in various research journals, websites, newspapers, and chapters in edited books. Her insights frequently feature in international print and broadcast media. Dr. Nivedita has augmented her expertise through additional qualifications. She holds a qualification in women, borders, and migration studies from the University of Hannover, Germany, and another in Eurasian Studies from the Pushkin Institute, Russia.

Her research interests revolve around geopolitics, foreign policy, security's strategic dimensions, multilateral organizations, as well as, women and migration issues. Her remarkable achievements include being awarded the prestigious state award "Pushkin Medal" in 2013. She has also been the recipient of esteemed fellowships, including DAAD (Germany), RAS (Russia), CIMO (European Union), ICSSR (India), and ADA (Azerbaijan). Notably, Dr. Nivedita Kundu is a member of the Chemical Weapons Convention Coalition, actively working on weapons of mass destruction (WMD) issues and concerns. She is a regular speaker at CSP-OPCW (UN) sessions held at The Hague.

Dr. Nivedita Das Kundu has recently become an Advisor for the expert working committee of the Shanghai Cooperation Organization SCO-TEMP (Trade and Economic Multifunctional Platform for SCO countries). Presently she is also a non-residential fellow and life member at the prestigious institutions such as the United Services Institution of India, Science for Peace- at University of Toronto, and the Valdai Discussion Club of Russia.

Brig Rahul K Bhonsle (Retd)

Brigadier Bhonsle, MSc, MPhil, MBA is an Indian army military veteran with 30 years of active field experience in counter-militancy and terrorism operations. Post-retirement since 2006, he has combined his military expertise with extensive study of future trends in conflict to build a personal repertoire of workshops, seminars, books, magazine and newspaper articles which are internationally acknowledged. He is presently the Director of Sasia Security-Risks.com, a South Asian security risk and knowledge management consultancy which specialises in future scenarios, military capacity building and conflict trends in South Asia. Brig Rahul Bhonsle has worked on the entire gamut of issues related to international security to include an overall assessment of non-traditional security threats to India as conceptualised in his 2004 book, "India's National Security: The Asymmetrical Challenges". His other book, "Securing India: Assessment of Defence and Security Capabilities" (2009) outlines defence modernisation strategies for India. His recent works related to terrorism include, "Beyond Bin Laden: Global Terrorism Scenarios," (2011) & "Countering Transnational Terrorism," (2010). A number of recommendations from these books have been incorporated in government policy on counter-terrorism in India. His website is www.security-risks.com

Group Captain Ajey Lele (Retd.)

Dr Ajay Lele is Senior Fellow at the Manohar Parrikar Institute for Defence Studies and Analyses (MP-IDSA) and heads its Centre on Strategic Technologies. He started his professional career as an officer in the Indian Air Force in 1987 and took early retirement from the service to pursue his academic interests. He has a Masters degree in Physics from Pune University, and Masters and MPhil degrees in Defence and Strategic Studies from Madras University. He has done his doctorate from the School of International Studies, Jawaharlal Nehru University (JNU), New Delhi. His specific areas of research include issues related to Weapons of Mass Destruction (WMD), Space Security and Strategic Technologies. He has contributed articles to various national and international journals, websites and newspapers. He has authored six books and has also has been an editor for six books. He is a recipient of K. Subrahmanyam Award (2013) which is conferred for outstanding contribution in the area of strategic and security studies.

Dr Roshan Khanijo

Dr Roshan is currently Assistant Director (Research) at the United Service Institution of India, New Delhi. Her academic qualifications include BSc, MA and PhD. Her area of interest is strategic issues, particularly Nuclear Strategy, Nuclear profile of Nuclear Weapon States, Armament, Disarmament, Niche technologies etc. She has authored and edited books, monographs, occasional papers namely, "Complexities and Challenges of Nuclear India", "The Indo-Pacific Region: Security Dynamics & Challenges", "Iranian Nuclear Conundrum", etc. She has been a panellist in various national and international panel discussions and a guest speaker at Air War College, Hyderabad, Southern Naval command, Kochi, OP Jindal Global University, etc. She was the member of the study team which did the Net Assessment on China, South Asia and Pakistan for HQ IDS, Ministry of Defence.

Dr. Pankaj K Jha

Dr Pankaj Jha is senior Associate Professor with Jindal School of International Affairs ,O P Jindal Global University. He is also Assistant Dean (Student Initiatives) and Editor–in–Chief of the Jindal Journal of International Affairs. He had worked as Director (Research) with Indian Council of World Affairs (ICWA) (2014-Feb 2017) and as the Deputy Director with National Security Council Secretariat (2012-2013), Prime Minister's Office.

Maj Gen BK Sharma, AVSM, SM** (Retd)

Maj Gen B K Sharma is currently the Director General of United Service Institution of India, New Delhi. He is PSC, HC, NDC, MPhil (Twice), and PGDM. His prestigious Command and Staff assignments include, Senior Faculty Member at NDC, New Delhi; Command of a Mountain Division, BGS of a Corps, Principal Director Net Assessment, Defence Attaché in Central Asia and UN Military Observer in Central America. He specialises in Strategic Net Assessment, Scenario Building and Strategic Gaming. He writes for professional journals and participates in national and international events.

Maj Gen S B Asthana, SM, VSM (Retd)

Gen Asthana is a globally acknowledged Strategic and Security Analyst who has authored over 400 publications. He is a veteran infantry General with 40 years of experience at national and varied international levels. He held various key appointments in Indian Army and the UN. He is also a TV commentator, speaker in various strategic, military forums, UN organisations and universities. He is regularly interviewed by various national and international news channels/newspapers/organisations on strategic, military and UN related subjects. Currently, he is on Governing/Security Council Confederation of Education Excellence CEE, International Organisation of Education Development (IOED), and other UN Organisations. He is also on the Advisory Board of Global Advisors Consultants Corporation, member Expert Group Challenges Forum, IOED representative in the UN Headquarters, Vienna, Austria. Gen Asthana is also a Chief Instructor at the USI of India, the oldest think tank of India.

He is former Director General, Infantry in Indian Army and distinguished expert at Bharat Centre of Canada. He has received awards twice by President of India, twice by UN and CEE excellence award for Nation building by Governor of Haryana. He was awarded for "International Diplomacy and Global Conflict Resolutions" by IOED twice, a Consultative body for ECOSOC and International Police Commission – IPC India, by former Prime Minister of Moldova.

Lt Gen GS Katoch, PVSM, AVSM, VSM (Retd.)

Lieutenant General GS Katoch, PVSM, AVSM, VSM (Retd.) is an infantry officer with nearly 40 years of service in the Army. He has extensive experience in counter-insurgency and counter-terrorist operations in J&K and North-East India. He has commanded an infantry battalion and brigade in Kashmir, an Infantry Division in the North-East and the India-China border and a Corps in the Desert Sector on the Western Front. He has two Masters Degrees, one in Defence & Strategic Studies from Madras University and the other in Defence Analysis with specialisation in Irregular Warfare from the Naval Postgraduate School, Monterey, California, USA. He also has an M. Phil in Defence & Strategic studies from Indore University. He is an alumnus of the National Defence College, India. He retired in March 2016 as the Director General Perspective Planning at the Army Headquarters which is the institutional think tank of the Indian Army. In that capacity he was also overseeing the Centre of Land Warfare Studies (CLAWS), the autonomous think tank of the Indian Army. He was the founding Director of The Centre for Anti-Terrorism Studies (CATS), at the National Security Guard (NSG).

Mr. Vijay Kranti

Vijay Kranti is a veteran journalist, Tibetologist and Chairman, Centre for Himalayan Asia Studies and Engagement 'CHASE'. He has a wide range of experience in Print Media, TV, Radio, Photography, Media Education, Corporate Communications and Corporate Social Responsibility. He has been on the staff of some leading media groups from India and abroad including India Today, BBC TV, Aaj Tak TV, Zee News TV, Deutsche Welle (German Radio) and Radio Voice of America. His main subject of specialisation is Tibet-China-India. For past four decades he has been keenly tracking and writing about political developments on Tibet and India-China relations. Mr Kranti has been a fellow of K.K. Birla Foundation for his work on Tibet as a journalist. He was the founding editor of monthly

'Tibbat-Desh', the only news magazine of its kind in Hindi from 1979 to 2010.

Brig Narender Kumar, SM, VSM (Retd.)

Brig Narender Kumar is an Infantry Officer with close to 15 years' experience in counter insurgency and anti-terrorism operations having served in Sri Lanka (Operation PAWAN) J&K and North East. He has been part of UN Mission in North Africa and also had a tenure in Indian Training Team in a foreign country. He has served as Brigade Major in Western Theatre, Col Administration of a Division and Brig General Staff of an Area responsible for Northern Border. He had also commanded a Rashtriya Rifles battalion in J&K and Assam Rifles Sector in North East.

Dr Muzaffar Hussain

Muzaffar Hussain is an Assistant Professor at the Department of Political Science, Maulana Azad National Urdu University (MANUU), Hyderabad. Before joining MANUU, he taught at Department of Political Science University of Delhi and School of Open Learning University of Delhi. He completed his Masters and Research Training from the School of International Studies, Jawaharlal Nehru University. He has also held several positions of responsibilities as Warden of Boys hostel MANUU, Coordinator of the Internal Quality Assurance Cell for the Department of Political Science MANUU, Coordinator of Lyceum Club, Department of Political Science, MANUU and Nodal Officer, Prime Minister Special Scholarship Programme, MANUU. He has written around 15 articles and his op-eds have appeared in newspapers and magazines like Tehelka, The Pioneer, State Times, Kashmir Times and Stawa. He has delivered five lectures as invited speaker in various workshops, courses and seminars.

Dr Raj Kumar Sharma

Dr Raj Kumar Sharma is currently Maharishi Kanad Post-Doc Fellow, Delhi School of Transnational Affairs, Institution of Eminence, University of Delhi. He holds a doctorate from School of International Studies, Jawaharlal Nehru University where he was a UGC-Senior Research Fellow. He is also a Research Fellow at the Bharat Centre for Canada. Dr Sharma has almost ten years of experience in media, think tank research and university teaching. His earlier appointments were at the Press Trust of India, New Delhi, United Service Institution of India, New Delhi, Indira Gandhi National Open University, New Delhi, Maitreyi College, University of Delhi and Rashtriya Raksha University, Gujarat. He has more than 50 publications including books, chapters in edited books, peer-reviewed articles, occasional papers, articles in UGC-approved journals, newspaper op-eds and online commentaries. Dr. Sharma also contributed to various Net Assessment studies on Pakistan, China, Bangladesh and Afghanistan conducted by USI for the Integrated Defence Staff (IDS), Ministry of Defence.

Abbreviations

ANI	Andaman and Nicobar Islands
APEC	Asia Pacific Economic Cooperation
ASEAN	Association of the South East Asian Nations
BBIN	Bangladesh, Bhutan, India, Nepal
BIMSTEC	Bay of Bengal Initiative for Multi-Sectoral Technical and Economic Cooperation
BRI	Belt and Road Initiative
C4ISR	Command, Control, Communications, Computer, Intelligence, Surveillance, and Reconnaissance
CAG	Comptroller and Auditor General
CAPF	Central Armed Police Forces
CBMs	Confidence Building Measures
CCP	Chinese Communist Party
CCS	Cabinet Committee on Security
CDS	Chief of Defence Staff
CMEC	China Myanmar Economic Corridor
CNEC	China Nepal Economic Corridor
CNP	Comprehensive National Power
CPC	Communist Party of China
CPEC	China Pakistan Economic Corridor
DRDO	Defence Research and Development Organisation
EEZ	Exclusive Economic Zone

ESA	European Space Agency
HADR	Humanitarian Assistance and Disaster Relief
IDA	Island Development Agency
IEA	International Energy Agency
IONS	Indian Ocean Naval Symposium
IOR	Indian Ocean Region
IORA	Indian Ocean Rim Association
IPEF	Indo-Pacific Economic Forum
JAXA	Japan Aerospace Exploration Agency
LAC	Line of Actual Control
LOC	Line of Control
MDA	Maritime Domain Awareness
MGC	Mekong Ganga Cooperation
NATO	North Atlantic Treaty Organisation
NFU	No First Use
NSA	National Security Advisor
NSS	National Security Strategy
PLA	People's Liberation Army
OIC	Organisation of Islamic Cooperation
RCEP	Regional Comprehensive Economic Partnership
SCO	Shanghai Cooperation Organisation
SCRI	Supply Chain Resilience Initiative
SLOCs	Sea Lanes of Communication
SSBN	Strategic Strike Nuclear Submarine
WMD	Weapons of Mass Destruction

Introduction

Nivedita Das Kundu

The Book on *India @ 75: Reflection on New India,* reflects on the creation of new India under the leadership of Prime Minister Narendra Modi. Narendra Modi Governments' first term was largely defined by campaigns like *Swachh Bharat* and *Beti Bachao, Beti Padhao (Save girl child, educate girl child).* Although, one can say that these campaigns have been age old catchphrases in India. However, the twist in these campaigns has been the stress on the use of technology and digital platforms to bring about the reforms. The sheer idea of digital India as a positive reinforcement made Narendra Damodardas Modi the epitome of change and reform.

During the first tenure of Narendra Modi from 2014 to 2019, Prime Minister Modi had many hits and misses. He was able to radically alter the country's arcane tax system and institute a comprehensible goods and services tax (GST). Additionally, by revamping the country's bankruptcy laws, he helped transform India into a serious destination for foreign investment and this moved up the country's ranking in the ease of doing business category as well. Significant infrastructure investment in roads, airports, public transportation and sanitation improved the lives of hundreds of millions of people in just a few years. Prime Minister Modi was able to channel India's gains from globalisation into actionable policy; for the first time in generations, India had a leader who seemed to transcend the country's sclerotic and corrupt politics to tangibly improve the lives of 'Aam Admi,' (common people). Through regular radio broadcasts, social media interactions, and personal appearances at hundreds of functions and rallies each year, Narendra Modi has successfully conveyed to the average Indian that new India's leader is sincere, hardworking and decisive. Even his policies that didn't pan out as expected—like pulling most of the country's hard currency out of circulation in an ill-fated attempt to quash the country's black market—still underscored that a leader was leading India with ambition and strategic vision.

Another event that captured the interest of the populace was the concept of surgical strikes. For quite long India's strategy with neighbours was termed as defensive and retaliatory while the Pulwama and Balakot Strike changed the entire narrative of India's defence posture, showcasing that India under Modi would adopt hardline stance whenever need be.

Prime Minister Modi is also a staunch believer in power technology and advocates that the country needs to adapt to the changing technological trends. Technology and digitalisation have also become the mainstays for his second term in office. A few reforms such as online application and processing, single-window clearances that remove the need to visit government offices often, speeding up of approvals, reduction of turnaround time across various domains were seen in a positive light during his first tenure. Even the number of procedures and documents needed to get any bureaucratic work done has been reduced remarkably. Aadhaar card system was brought in as a one stop solution to managing several document problems. Ayushman Bharat Yojna that is currently underway, has made healthcare as a primary focus area for the country such that the basic medicines and treatments could reach to the grassroots level of the society. In continuation of its policy of India's technological makeover, Prime Minister Modi has inaugurated the first Undersea Optical Fibre Cable Project for Andaman and Nicobar Islands optical fibre project. This project aims to provide high-speed broadband connections in the Andaman and Nicobar Islands which would not only boost the local economy but also facilitate the delivery of e-governance, telemedicine, and tele-education.

Modi 2.0 strategy has also continued to focus the political energies on socio-political issues like ending the temporary special status of Kashmir, doing away with triple talaq, fast-tracking citizenship for regional minorities through the Citizenship Amendment Bill, and starting the Ram Mandir construction. On the geostrategic front, the government has been focused on strengthening connectivity in the IOR (Indian Ocean Region) region, while balancing China and the United States of America.

This book aims to analyse new India's policy's under the leadership of PM Modi, underlining the challenges that continue to constrain New Delhi's choices. The book is a comprehensive survey of geopolitical, geostrategic and technological policy landscape over the past few years, acknowledging the achievements and underscoring the continuing challenges facing the nation's policymakers.

One of the crucial moves of the government was the abrogation of Article 370 provisions. This decision was seen as a necessity to integrate Jammu and Kashmir (J&K) fully into the Republic of India. In fact a year after the revocation of Jammu and Kashmir's special status, the Ministry of Home Affairs (MHA) in its report has noted a 36 per cent decline in the number of terror activities.[1] Furthermore, the book underscores the salience of Modi's defence policy, the change in the prevailing narrative of the country that has been characterised by surgical strikes and ASAT (Anti-satellite weapon test) testing and the emerging geostrategic environment. The government has also worked on reforming the higher defence management by creating the post of Chief of Defence Staff (CDS). The creation of this position has been a long-pending demand and is expected to enhance jointness (defined as the ability of the army, air force, and navy to operate together) and provide coherence to overall defence policy. The CDS will prioritise requirements of the three services within budgetary allocations, taking a big responsibility away from the ministry, and has also been tasked to facilitate "restructuring of military commands for optimal utilisation of resources by bringing about jointness in operations, including through the establishment of joint/theatre commands". That is an important role, which also points to a reform roadmap for the future — towards the eventual creation of joint theatre commands.[2] With the decision, Modi seems intent on transforming the Indian military. New India has been forecasted to focus on strengthening deterrence by building medium to long term capability. Prime Minister's clarion call of 'Atmanirbhar Bharat' (self-reliant India), aims at building a more resilient and prosperous India. In this context, the government has recently raised the Foreign Direct Investment (FDI) cap in the defence sector to 74 per cent and two defence corridors are going to be set up to encourage the production of defence equipment.[3]

Rapid adaption and adoption of science and technology policies have been a driving force during Prime Minister Modi's tenure and the government's continuous perseverance to fill the technology gap so as to achieve the goal of becoming USD 5 Trillion Economy can be seen in many initiatives. The book also addresses the China issue by shedding light on the country's foray in the South Asian region and its implications for India. The recent India-China standoff that took place across multiple points in Ladakh indicates a high degree of Chinese premeditation and approval of its activities from the very top of the Chinese leadership. China's growing assertive strategic behavior has raised significant concerns for India as well as, the international community. In this context, India has already banned over 100 Chinese mobile applications and its clones, changed the rules to bar Chinese firms from getting government contracts. The country is also taking sustained measures to pave the way for effective strategic dialogue so as to strengthen peace and prosperity between the two neighbours.

The book also notes the importance of the Andaman and Nicobar Islands in India's Maritime Strategy. Considering the security of Indo-Pacific has seen a rise in both traditional and non-traditional threats. In future, the waters of the Indian Ocean are going to get more congested with conventional and nuclear assets and brinkmanship will increase. In such a scenario, Andaman and Nicobar Islands would play a crucial role.

In the last few years, India has transformed and modernised from being merely an important player in the global order into one that is willing—and able—to define the priorities of the international system. Modi's first tenure was largely seen as the harbinger of new foreign policy measures — from restructuring the Look East Policy to Act East Policy (which aims to connect India to East Asia through better infrastructure, trade and regional institutions) and managing the periphery of pacific as well as, commitment towards the Indo-Pacific construct was seen as a welcome change in the Indian context. Without taking a defined position on the contested power politics in the Indo-Pacific, India has always maintained cordial relations with most countries and stakeholders in the region. As a corollary to this, the rubric of Security and Growth for All in the Region (SAGAR) advances India's maritime diplomacy in the Indo-Pacific, reflecting India's desire to manage maritime security and governance in the Indian Ocean Region (IOR).

The Modi government continues to redefine India's foreign policy priorities, both in substance and style, while showcasing India's aspiration to become a leading power, rather than just a balancing power. The Modi government managed to lay out a worldview that did away with many of the banalities of the past and there is a renewed focus on pragmatic engagements in the realm of foreign affairs.

All these developments surely point towards some positive traction that the present Modi government gained so far during its tenure. Thus, the challenges remain equally significant as the Modi government looks at operationalising its ideas into policy. This is especially true at a time when New Delhi is being required to respond to a major disruption, caused due to COVID-19 and Russia-Ukraine war, there is a desperate need to get the Indian economy back on track. At the same time, the global order is evolving at a pace which will only get more difficult to navigate. Amidst the global pandemic, Russia-Ukraine war, economic recession and competing national interests, there is a need for a comprehensive framework to generate revenues and boost economies. India will have to sustain its growing global footprint to enjoy any credibility as a leading global power. Its ability to deliver on the ground will get scrutinised even more now that it wants to shoulder greater global responsibilities. It is yet to be seen how the Modi government is going to combat these herculean tasks and still emerge victorious in coming years.

This book is divided into four sections. The first section is about *Recent Trends in India-China Relations*, the second section presents about the *Science, Technology and Military Modernisation* of India, the third section attempts to analyse *perspectives from Indian Ocean and Indo-Pacific*, the fourth section is on *Internal Dynamics*. Overall the chapters in this volume touched upon various aspects on New India. The theme of the chapters dexterously worked out with well-documented data based on the sources. This edited volume has the potential to provide a broad idea and clarity on the crucial topic under study. The readers will find important information and understanding about India @ 75 in this volume. The book will provide readers with different viewpoints on different topics. It is expected that the book will provide useful inputs to policy planners and researchers.

Endnotes

1   Manish Shukla, "Terror Activities Reduced Significantly in Kashmir after Abrogation of Article 370: Union Ministry of Home Affairs Report," *ZEE News,* 29 July 2020, available at https://zeenews.india.com/india/terror-activities-reduced-significantly-in-kashmir-after-abrogation-of-article-370-union-ministry-of-home-affairs-report-2299216.html, accessed on 13 August 2020.

2   "Towards Jointness," *The Indian Express,* 26 December 2019, available at https://indianexpress.com/article/opinion/editorials/chief-of-defence-staff-army-navy-air-force-towards-jointness-6184809/, accessed on 02 August 2020.

3   "To Attract more Investors, PM Modi cites India's high FDI Cap in Defence, Space" *Hindustan Times,* 22 July 2020, available at https://www.hindustantimes.com/india-news/to-attract-more-investors-pm-modi-cites-india-s-high-fdi-cap-in-defence-space/story-4T12iigSSrbPek2zX0YEdO.html, accessed on 07 August 2020.

Section I

Recent Trends in India-China Relations

Chapter 1

China's Strategic Forays in South Asia and Indian Ocean: Implications for India

B K Sharma

Introduction

Lee Kuan Yew, founding father and first Prime Minister of Singapore had observed in globally-acknowledged *Grand Master's Insights on China, the United States and the World*: "It is China's intention to be the greatest power in the world. In Chinese, China means Middle Kingdom – recalling a world in which they were dominant in the region and other states related to them as supplicants".[1] China's strategic outlook is shaped by her ancient strategic culture and contemporary geopolitical imperatives. Her profound self-concept of grandiose is anchored in the 'Middle Kingdom' mind-set. *The Classics of History*, a document of the 6th century BC, visualised the world in four major concentric geographical zones emanating from the seat of power – the Royal Domains, a Pacification Zone, the Zone of Allied Barbarians and the Zone of Savagery.[2] Paradoxically, the 'Century of Humiliation' punctuated this outlook.[3]

In Chinese thinking, subjugation by colonial powers in the 19th century has been an aberration in the shining historical past of their great civilisation. Mao perceived the world through a prism of 'three world theory', namely imperialists, revisionists and international proletariats, and in terms of three adversaries as arch-rivals, secondary enemies and potential enemies, arrayed against the revolutionary force.[4] The present leadership categorises relations with countries as friendly, neutral and rival. Therefore, China's contemporary self–concept is shaped by a sense of past grandeur, a bruised psyche and the perception that the rest of the world is inimical to China's rise. The slogans of unfinished historical agenda and China Dream allude to the revival of her past glory and the integration of Taiwan, consolidation of territories within the *Nine Dash Line* and cartographic assertion on the border with India.

China's assertive strategic behaviour has raised significant international concern. China's core leader Xi Jinping is assiduously working to create an alternate security and economic architecture with Beijing in the leadership role. A well-enunciated *China Dream* that seeks to build the country into a *Great Power* by 2050 coincides with 100 years of the existence of People's Republic of China (PRC). The Belt and Road Initiative (BRI) is Beijing's de-facto grand strategy that seeks to connect continents and oceans through multi–modal connectivity and strings of economic zones to expand China's strategic influence in the world. The most significant feature of BRI are the four transit corridors spanning Eurasia and the China Pakistan Economic Corridor (CPEC), China-Myanmar Economic Corridor (CMEC) and China–Nepal Economic Corridor (CNEC) that meander through India's western and northern flanks. A vital web of Maritime Silk Route (MSR) spans the Indian Ocean. Gwadar Port in the Arabian Sea and Kyaukphyu Port in the Bay of Bengal have emerged as the strategic outposts, where the continental and maritime prongs of the BRI converge. China's growing influence in Myanmar, South Asia and the IOR (Indian Ocean Region) is rapidly changing the geopolitical landscape of the region and consequently shifting the balance of power in China's favor. These geopolitical developments have a profound impact on India's strategic interests in the region.

Geopolitical Imperatives that Shape China's Strategic Outlook

Three geopolitical imperatives shape China's strategic security outlook. First is the prosperity of the Chinese Han agriculturist heartland, where one billion Han agriculturists suffer from a relative sense of deprivation.[5] Development of the Heartland is a major socio-economic challenge for the Communist Party of China (CPC). From ancient times, the ruling regimes were brought down by a combination of internal dissonance and external abetment. The collapse of the Ming Dynasty in 1644 was caused after rebelling peasants took Beijing and the Manchu with the collusion of Ming generals invading from the north. Manchu's own Qing dynasty fell 300 years later after a series of internal conflicts coincided with Western and Japanese Invasions.[6] From the writer's interaction with Chinese thinkers during visit to Chengdu in September 2018, it was apparent that China is concerned that a pushback on the BRI will cause socio-economic stress in the country and impinge on the credibility of Xi Jinping as a core leader. There is a muted debate about Xi Jinping's decision to do away with Deng's Collective Leadership Model as he has now become China's supreme leader for life. The debate is also on the effect of the US economic sanctions and that sustained economic sanctions over $ 400 billion could reduce China's GDP, cause loss of millions of jobs, trigger labour migrations to urban areas and result in social tensions. The uprising in Hong Kong is posing the biggest sovereignty challenge to China since the days of infamous quelling of June 1989 Tiananmen Square uprising. China's endeavour of reunification under the "One Country Two Systems" framework is facing strong headwinds in Hong Kong. These developments do not augur well for nudging Taiwan towards unification; Taipei has already adopted a strident position vis-à-vis mainland China with overt support from the US. Hong Kong protests and the Taiwan unification have emerged as major challenges for the Chinese Communist Party (CCP).

The second geopolitical imperative is that of restive non–Han *buffer* region comprising Xinjiang, Tibet, Inner Mongolia and Manchuria that accounts for about 60 percent of Chinese territory but is inhabited only by seven percent of its population. Historically, these *buffer* regions have been under Chinese rule whenever China was strong and broke away when China was weak. Hence, Beijing's emphasis on the Unity of Motherland and China's security concerns regarding her strategic periphery pertain to the threat from the Three Evils–"Separatism, Extremism and Terrorism". The unrest in Xinjiang province, which is the geographical fountainhead of BRI, has profound impact on China's strategic interests. The Uighurs in China number about 8 million, which is less than one percent of China's population, but they account for 45 percent of Xinjiang's population. The impetus to economic growth and social re-engineering has not been able to assuage sub-national sentiments in Xinjiang. China has reportedly imposed very stringent curbs on the religious freedom and put one million people in reformation camps.[7] These measures have attracted worldwide condemnation of China for human rights violations. Control over East Turkestan Islamic Movement and denial of space to them in Pakistan,

Afghanistan and Central Asia is a central feature of China's regional periphery strategy. Stability in Xinjiang is critical for the success of CPEC, which is a bone of contention between India and China.

Mao termed Tibet as China's palm with five fingers extending as Arunachal Pradesh, Sikkim, Bhutan, Nepal and Ladakh.[8] Tibet figures prominently in China's strategic calculus. It is the tower of Asia, rich in resources and shares vast borders with India, Nepal and Bhutan. China has adopted a two-pronged strategy to assimilate Tibet. One is the massive development of the region and the second, social re-engineering of the Tibetan population. Robert Kaplan writes in Foreign Affairs (2011), "Without Tibet China would be but a rump and India would add another zone to its sub-continental powerbase".[9] China's water resources are skewed, with 81 percent of water resources located in relatively less populated northern areas and only 19 percent of water resources available in the high population density areas of the South. Assimilation of Tibet continues to be a cause of concern for Beijing.

China has done away with the system of adopting Lamaism at a young age. Children cannot go to seminaries till they have acquired formal education up to 12th standard (18 years of age) in government schools. Also, the Chinese have put their own people in the management of Buddhist shrines, who ensure a strict overview of how these shrines are run. From author's impression during Tibet visit in 2018, it was clear that the effect of social re-engineering is manifest in the streets of Lhasa, where more youth are attired in swanky attire playing with their smart phones than dressed in traditional costumes with their fingers on the beads. The issue of the succession of the Dalai Lama is a potential flash point that could impact Sino-Indian relations. In Tibet, China has improved rail-road connectivity, military airfields, signal communication and oil pipelines. A large number of logistics hubs with underground facilities have been constructed to achieve 'Single Season Military Campaign' capability against India. As per author's study and observations as a military divisional commander deployed opposite Tibet in Sikkim and visit to Tibet in 2018, China now regularly conducts trans-regional support operations military mobilisation, logistics and fire drills in Tibet.

The most important geopolitical imperative for China is the security of its coastal areas – the country's economic centers of gravity. Maritime geography in the Western Pacific region imposes a kind of siege mentality on China. Taiwan is a strategic pivot in the Western Pacific that abuts the East China Sea and South China Sea. Macarthur aptly described Taiwan as an "unsinkable carrier".[10] China's claims in East China Sea are based on historical basis and on the 'Principal of Extended Continental Shelf', which extends beyond 200 Nautical Miles (NM) limit. China claims 80 percent of Social Credit System (SCS) based on a 'Nine Dash Claim-line'. The issue of contested sovereignty in the two seas with Japan, Philippines, Vietnam and some other states and the vulnerability of the Western and the Eastern Sea line of communication (SLOC) markedly shape China's threat perception. This strategic reality explains China's Taiwan sensitivity, the oft-repeated Malacca Dilemma'[11] and the growing security concerns over the US Indo-Pacific strategy. The aforesaid security calculus drives China's "Two Ocean and Counter Intervention Strategy".[12] The Indian Ocean is part of the two oceans that China wants to dominate, the other being the Pacific. Hence, China's hectic port-building activities in India's perceived sphere of influence are emerging as a potential friction point between the two countries.

South Asia and the Indian Ocean in China's Strategic Calculus

South Asia and Indian Ocean Region (IOR) assume added importance in China's strategic calculus from the perspective of securing her regional periphery, combating the three evils to her security, gaining access to the Indian Ocean region and restraining India – the only potential competitor in the region. China perceives India as part of the 'Grand Encirclement Design' being weaved by the US to contain her rise. India is deemed to be a competitor in the IOR and South Asia, vying for domination of strategic resources, locations and influence. China is pursuing a well-crafted twin strategy of balancing India in the IOR and South Asia. This strategy is manifest in her endeavors to alter the geopolitical and security landscape of the region along India's continental borders and maritime boundary and at the same time engage India, thus preventing New Delhi from binding with the US. The key Chinese endeavors that impact India are discussed in the succeeding paragraphs.

Pakistan-China Strategic Nexus

Pakistan is a lynchpin in China's South Asia strategy. The two countries have romanticised this relationship by a cliché: "higher than mountain, deeper than ocean, stronger than steel". Foreign policy mandarins in Beijing have coined a new epithet for Pakistan – "Ba Taa, the Iron brother". The Pakistan–China strategic partnership is essentially an asymmetric relationship. Noted former Pakistan diplomat Hussain Haqqani, says that for China, Pakistan is a low-cost secondary deterrence to India".[13] For Pakistan, China is a high value guarantor of security against India. President Xi Jinping, during his April 2015 visit to Islamabad had alluded, "China will be Pakistan's net security provider". Rawalpindi plays the "Dragon card" to pose a two-front dilemma for India while it prosecutes proxy war in Kashmir with impunity. China is the major supplier of military hardware and nuclear technology to Pakistan. CPEC[14], the strategic flagship program of Xi Jinping's signature' BRI Initiative, has further cemented their strategic embrace. This corridor passes through the northern areas of Pakistan-Occupied Kashmir. China has become de-facto a third party in the Kashmir dispute since it is in illegal occupation of Aksai Chin and Shaksgam Valley, which are legally part of India's territory.

Myanmar

It is the strategic pivot where India and China's strategic interests intersect. China signed an Memorandum of Understanding (MoU) with Myanmar in September 2018 to develop the multi–modal China Myanmar Economic Corridor (CMEC) that encompasses construction of $1.5 billion oil and gas pipeline, $1.3 billion for first stage expansion of Kyaukphyu Port and $2.7 billion for developing 4,000 acre SEZ (Special Economic Zone) with 70 percent stake of CITIC Group of China (International Trust Investment Corporation). Besides, a 1400 km high speed railway line is planned. As part of the ambitious BRI project, China is keen to develop Muse-Mandalay Railway Project, create the New Yangon Development Project costing $1.5 billion (setting up modern towns and industrial parks), three Border Economic Zones and revival of the shelved Myitsone hydropower project worth $3.6 billion. As of 2023 China is involved in developing 126 projects worth $ 15 billion. China has a 30-year perspective to invest in Myanmar in hydropower projects, mining sector, energy pipelines, deep sea port, industrial and Information Technology (IT) parks and the agriculture sector. China is developing a road on the Kunming-Myitkyina-Pangsau pass on the India-Myanmar border, and also the road from Kunming to Bangkok. It plans to develop a railway line from Jinhong in Yunnan province to Vientiane in Thailand.

Nepal and Bhutan

China wants to develop the China-Nepal Economic Corridor. Among the multitude of Chinese projects in Nepal, the vital ones are – one railway, two highways, two airports, three border ports, the Lhasa-Kathmandu railway and the Gyirong and Zhangmu land border port projects. The moot point is can India afford to have an open border with Nepal. The impact of China's influence on the regional economy and security of the Siliguri corridor needs detailed examination. The Siliguri corridor is a critical gateway to north-eastern Indian states which share international border with Myanmar, Bangladesh, Nepal, Bhutan and Tibet. China is assiduously working to lure Bhutan with a package deal. China is prepared to forego its territorial claims in eastern Bhutan if Thimphu accedes to China's claim over 269 sq km in western Bhutan (including 89 sq km of Doklam plateau) and open diplomatic and trade relations between the two countries, as per author's impressions from discussions with officials of Bhutan during visits in 2009 and 2011. The signing of MoU between China and Bhutan to solve their border dispute is an indication that India needs to be cautious in this regard.

Bangladesh, Sri Lanka and Maldives

Bangladesh, Sri Lanka and Maldives are the signatories of MSR (Molten Salt Reactor Project). In Bangladesh, China has invested in about 27 projects, evinced interest in Chittagong and Payra port, in creating an SEZ at Anwara, apart from developing power plants, railway and road networks, bridges and oil pipelines. The bilateral trade between China and Bangladesh in fiscal year 2023 was around US $12 billion. In Sri Lanka, China has developed Colombo container terminal worth $1.4 billion, Colombo financial city Hambantota port, power projects, road and rail connectivity and SEZ. Likewise, Chinese projects in Maldives entail airport expansion, construction of Friendship Bridge, lease of Feydhoo Finolhu for 50 years at $4 million, setting up an ocean observation station at Makunudhu and development of the port at Laamu Atoll. It may be mentioned that Sri Lanka in 2021 has scrapped a trilateral agreement involving India and Japan investments to develop the strategic East Container Terminal (ECT) at the Colombo Port.

Indian Ocean Region Littorals

Development of ports is the cornerstone of China's IOR strategy.[15] The major ports of interest are Gwadar/Jiwani in Pakistan, Colombo Terminal and port City, Hambantota in Sri Lanka, Payra Port in Bangladesh, Kyaukpyu port in Myanmar, Melaka Gateway Project and Kuantan Port in Malaysia, Khalifa Port in UAE, Aden Container Port and Mokha Container Port in Yemen, Dolareh port in Djibouti, Mombasa and Lamuports in Kenya, Dar-es-Salaam and Bagamoyo Port in Tanzania, Beira Fishing Port, Narinda Bay Port and Techobanine Ports in Mozambique. China is also eyeing Chittagong Port in Bangladesh, Gadhoo Port in Maldives and Kra Isthumus Canal in Thailand. As per experts, these ports are being developed as bridgeheads for political and military purposes by the People's Republic of China (PRC) owned and politically linked private firms to create a network of logistics facilities – "first commercial and then military use". There is a need to closely monitor China's maritime activities such as surveys, explorations, setting up of in situ recovery and communication facilities for maritime domain awareness, port calls and naval exercises culminating into establishment of rotational/permanent naval bases.

India-China Relations

India-China relations are characterised by the three Cs: Cooperation, Competition and Conflict. The two countries show conditional cooperation in the arena of global commons and reformation of international institutions, except that China opposes Indian candidature for permanent seat at the UNSC (United National Security Council) and entry into NSG (Nuclear Supply Group). Earlier, China supported Pakistan to scuttle UN resolution 1267 to declare Mohammad Azhar as an international terrorist. Post revocation of Article 370 by India, China has raised objections to the creation of Ladakh as a Union Territory. It has also supported Pakistan to raise the Kashmir issue at the UNSC.

The two countries are natural competitors in the Asian strategic space for access to resources, domination of locations and influence. If the two countries are unable to manage their competition, they could drift towards a conflictive course with issues such as boundary dispute, Tibet, and accidental standoff in the IOR as potential triggers, exacerbated by mistrust devolving around the Indo-US proximity, the Sino-Pak nexus and the water sharing issue. The Biden administration would continue to question China's policies, whether economic or security and after the American withdrawal from Afghanistan, the US is planning to focus more on the China challenge. Simultaneously, China's Hong Kong and Taiwan challenge has exacerbated. At present, the primary contradiction for China is how to deal with the US on these issues. For now, India is perceived as a secondary contradiction. Beijing can ill-afford two major Asian powers, viz. Japan and India to ally with Washington. A strategic alliance like the Quad, if successful, could impede China becoming a developed country by 2035 and a superpower by 2049, as envisaged in "China Dream". The AUKUS alliance will add to China's strategic headache and would benefit India as Quad and AUKUS are likely to complement each other in their joint effort to balance China.

China is cognizant of India's growing economic heft and resolve to protect its core interests. India's stand during the military face-offs at Doklam, Chumar and Depsang over the last few years and the ongoing border standoff in Ladakh, and continued reservations about the BRI – particularly its flagship project, the CPEC, has made China realise that it is premature to coerce India. Realpolitik on the part of China demands a tactical adjustment to steer relations with India to a manageable level till the American challenge is mitigated. From a broader perspective, the irreconcilable differences in the strategic objectives of the two powers suggest that their emerging bonhomie won't mask their deeper differences for long. At the 14th National People's Conference, President Xi exhorted the People's Liberation Army not to lose even an inch of China's territory.

China's strident position on the disputed border with India, on the Tibet issue as well as the fact that it has become a de facto third party in the Kashmir imbroglio means that any breakthrough in the boundary dispute will remain elusive. Efforts to obtain tangible assurances on not diverting the waters of the Brahmaputra River, correcting the enormous trade imbalance and India's membership of NSG have so far yielded little gain. China's outreach into South Asia and the IOR is inducing a gravitational pull-on India's neighbouring states.

India's Strategy under PM Modi to Balance China

India's world view is steeped in the ancient dictum '*Vasudhaiva Kutumbakam*' (the world is one family). The tenets of the NDA government can be summarised as the transformation of India from a balancing power to a leading power, creation of a conducive external environment for India's comprehensive national development, respect for international laws and pursuance of an interest-based multi-vector alignment. After assuming power, Prime Minister Modi has articulated the epithet NARA (National Ambition and Regional Aspiration), and reinforced his regional vision SAGAR (Security and Growth for All in the Region). India's Neighborhood First, Connect Central Asia Policy, Go West Policy and Act East policy are articles of this expression.

The new India looks at Indo-Pacific cooperation not as a camp to contain another country but to work under the international norms for a shared future of comity of nations. India's Act East Policy provides it a critical window to expand and deepen relations with South Asian neighbors, Indian Ocean littorals and South East Asia. Speedy operationalisation of the *Act East Policy* is a sine qua non to balance China in South Asia and IOR. India must expediently address security and development issues in the northeast, deepen engagement with Myanmar and assume a leadership role in shaping the strategic environment in the IOR. Myanmar is the gateway to Southeast Asia. Completion of the multi-modal Kaladan project and the Tri-lateral highway from India to Myanmar, Laos and Thailand is a strategic imperative for India. Likewise, Andaman and Nicobar should be transformed into a maritime strategic hub. Direct trade with Aceh province of Indonesia and setting up a Joint Working Group to develop Sabang Port in Indonesia are steps in the right direction. The recent economic problems in South Asian countries like Sri Lanka, Nepal and Pakistan are grim reminders to these countries that too much proximity with Beijing would bring economic costs and it may be beneficial for them to rectify their foreign and economic policy posture. India has stood by its commitments to its neighbours under its neighbourhood first policy during recent tough times and would continue to do so.

India's intent to harness blue economy and be a net security provider in the non-traditional security domain needs a concerted push. India has revamped cooperation on Maritime Domain Awareness, is helping littorals in networking coastal surveillance systems and has entered White Shipping Agreements with various stakeholders. India's contribution in the Indian Ocean Rim Association (IORA) and Indian Ocean Naval Symposium (IONS) is well-acclaimed. These frameworks offer scope for enhancing maritime security and developing blue economy in the Indian

Ocean with India in the leadership role. There are promising prospects in integrating Delhi-Mumbai-Bengaluru-Chennai with regional corridors, BBIN initiative and BIMSTEC (Bay of Bengal Initiative for Multi-Sectoral Technical and Economic Cooperation), develop ports as part of the Sagarmala project, establish free trade agreements in the IOR and revive maritime historical routes. Apart from reviving the "Cotton Route" with Central Asia, India plans to launch project *"Mausam"*, a regional initiative to revive its ancient maritime routes and cultural linkages with countries in the extended neighbourhood. Comprehensive capacity building, deft diplomacy in strengthening strategic bilateral and multi-lateral engagements and offering alternate models of growth and development to neighbours will attract other countries to join partnerships with India for balancing China.

Conclusion

India and China are two major Asian countries that must work in tandem to realise the dream of the Asian Century. A new *modus vivendi* between China and India is a strategic imperative to build peace and prosperity. New Delhi should be deft and steadfast in making Beijing understand and heed India's core interests and sensitivities, particularly about terrorism and the behaviour of Pakistan. The two sides must embark upon a sustained strategic dialogue to build trust and make bilateral relations interdependent and complementary. In the meantime, India should build capacities to reclaim strategic influence in South Asia and IOR, and place itself in a favourable position for a long-term balance of power. India must develop credible deterrence capabilities to secure its borders against any external aggression. Concurrently, measures to build strategic trust, complementarities and interdependence with China must continue with dignity and sincerity.

Endnotes

1   Allison, Graham , Blackwill, D & Wyne, Ali. (2012). *Lee Kuan Yew: The Grand Master's Insights on China, United States and the World*. London. MIT Press.

2   Jacques, Martin. (2009). *When China Rules the World: The End of the Western World and Birth of New Global World Order*. London. Pengain Books Ltd.

3   Jingxian, Lu. (2019). Is China still haunted by century of humiliation?. *Global Times*. January 6. Accessed September 22, 2021, http://www.globaltimes.cn/content/1134710.shtml

4   Zedong, Mao. (1974). *On the Question of the Differentiation of the Three Worlds*. Accessed September 23, 2021, https://www.revolutionarydemocracy.org/rdv10n1/mao.htm

5   Stratfor. (2013). *The Geopolitics of the Yangtze River: Developing the Interior*. Accessed September 23, 2021, https://worldview.stratfor.com/article/geopolitics-yangtze-river-developing-interior

6   Jisi,Wang. (2011). China's Search for a Grand Strategy. *Foreign Affairs*. March /April 2011.

7   Amnesty International. (2018). Up to one million detained in China's mass re-education drive. September 24, 2021, https://www.amnesty.org/en/latest/news/2018/09/china-up-to-one-million-detained/

8   Chatterjee, Ajoy. (2011). Liberation of Tibet's Five Fingers. September 24, 2021, www.globalpolitician.com

9   Kaplan, Robert D. (2010). The Geography of Chinese Power: How Far Can Beijing Reach on Land and at Sea?. *Foreign Affairs*. Vol. 89, No. 3 (May/June 2010), pp. 22-41.

10 Mazza, Michael. (2011). Why Taiwan Maters. *American Enterprise Institute*. Accessed September 27, 2021, http://thedeplomate.com/china-power/why-taiwan-matters/

11 Tunningley, James. (2017). *Can China overcome the Malacca Dilemma through OBOR and CPEC?*. Accessed September 28, 2021, https://globalriskinsights.com/2017/03/china-overcome-malacca-dilemma-obor-cpec/

12 Nantulya, Paul. (2015). *On Chinese Strategy: "Counter intervention" in substance but not in name is still "Counter intervention"*. Accessed September 28, 2021, https://strategicdepth.org/2015/08/21/counter-intervention-in-substance-but-not-

13   Sharma, B K. (2019). *Determinants of Pakistan China Strategic Nexus: Strategic Implication for India*. Accessed September 28, 2021, https://bharatshakti.in/determinants-of-pakistan-china-strategic-nexus-strate

14   Krishnan, Ananth. (2013). China- Pakistan Deal on Economic Corridor passing Through POK. *The Hindu*. May 23.

15   Sharma, B K. (2019b). *Net Assessment of China's Strategic Forays in India's Neighbourhood*. Accessed September 29, 2021, https://bharatshakti.in/net-assessme

Chapter 2

Chinese 'Concirclement' of India and Standoff: Way Ahead

Shashi Asthana

Background

Currently, the global attention is towards Russia-Ukraine War, wherein US led NATO projects Russian offensive against Ukraine, as a breach of the territorial integrity of a sovereign democratic country by a hegemon. China on the other hand, hasn't faced global ire despite incremental encroachment of territories of many sovereign democratic countries in Asian neighbourhood. Some examples are annexation of Tibet, Aksai Chin and EEZ of many South China Sea countries. China has a long-term strategy to dislodge the US as a superpower by 2049 or earlier, but regionally, it wants a China-centric Asia, for which containment of other regional players like India is a pre-requisite. To achieve that, besides land grabbing activities by incremental encroachment, it is creating bases (String of Pearls) and corridors like China-Pakistan Economic Corridor (CPEC) and China Myanmar Economic Corridor (CMEC) which amount to encircling India. The land grab by such activities has often led to many standoffs, including the current one in Eastern Ladakh, which seems to be vanishing from global memory amidst fresh global challenges. China, however, continues to build infrastructure in encroached land like the second bridge on Pangong Tso recently, additional camps and villages along Line of Actual Control (LAC), which is a major concern for India, posing a grave challenge to resolve it, preferably without any military action in the interest of regional peace and stability. This chapter explains the Chinese 'concirclement' of India, focusing on the ongoing Ladakh standoff and possible options for India.

Strategic 'Concirclement'

Unchallenged Xi Jinping with the renewed mandate by CCP, during his conversation with President Joe Biden, has tried to create an impression of bipolar world order in existence, although the rest of the world amidst Covid-19 pandemic continues its rebalancing between unipolar, bipolar and multipolar global order as per their perception. If Beijing has its way, it will use all instruments of power (ethical and unethical) to be the sole superpower at the global stage and have China-centric Asia at regional stage, at the earliest, for which sub-ordination of India is considered essential. To achieve the containment plus encirclement (concirclement) of India is a strategic necessity to be able to coerce it to China-centric alignment, preferably without undertaking contact warfare. Chanakya's wisdom that a neighbour with unsettled border can never be a friend seems to have been realised by New Delhi, which has been consistently involved in talkathon with China for decades hoping to have friendly neighbour. India needs to work out options in all domains, in fragile international environment, to undertake China challenge to avoid concirclement, preserve its sovereignty and territorial integrity, besides continuing its own march towards becoming a strong pole in global order.

Multidimensional 'Concirclement' of India by China

In the absence of any border treaty between Independent India and China and non-demarcated Line of Actual Control (LAC), the standoffs will continue. The present one in Eastern Ladakh seems to have run into a stalemate, to India's disadvantage, especially due to shortage of leverages, although India refuses to be coerced to resume business as usual side-lining border/LAC issue and insists on further pull back of People's Liberation Army (PLA) from all friction points to lead to de-escalation. China wants to avoid further pull back as it continues building additional infrastructure to upgrade its encroachment into areas it was not supposed to occupy as per Confidence Building Measures (CBMs), as permanent settlements. Chinese aim is to label it as settlement of border issue, somewhat in consonance with its 1959/60 claim line in strategically important areas. With occasional intrusions in other areas along LAC, China is trying to increase the economic cost of deployment for India by turning the LAC into similar situation that persists along Line of Control (with Pakistan) and stretching out Indian Military to seek Sino-centric solution.

The 'Containment Strategy' of China includes planned construction of 628 dual use, border defence villages along its own perception of LAC to provide permanency to its claim, enhance its ISR capabilities (some of which have already been made), providing it infrastructure like fibre optic connection, akin to outposts. China can claim that its Land Borders Law[1] passed recently by National People's Congress is applicable to all countries, but the timing suggests it to be part of containment of India. The law improves coordination between agencies and power to defend increasingly claimed land under garb of national integrity. China's recent MOU with Bhutan for resolving border issues bilaterally and allurement of Nepal are also steps towards containment of India. A possible Chinese gain at Doklam through a land swap with Bhutan from other areas can be a serious concern for India due to its proximity to Siliguri Corridor. China has also encroached to make villages in both these countries.

The aggressiveness in 'Encirclement Strategy' is evident from China delivering – most advanced frigates/warships to Pakistan. Labelled as gift, India must take it as cover plan for deployment of its People's Liberation Army (Navy) (PLAN) combat ships in Pakistan territorial water/Arabian sea, perhaps under Pakistan flag, adding another pearl to its ongoing 'String of Pearl Strategy'. Gwadar port as part of CPEC, China Myanmar Economic Corridor leading to Bay of Bengal and foothold in Sri Lanka and Bangladesh are part of overall encirclement plan of India. The most worrying part for India is Chinese encroachment in non-contact warfare domain. Chinese increasing economic, technological and digital offensive against India and other countries have made them so dependent on China, denting their self-reliance, so that the responses to Chinese unethical encroachment get muted. Chinese strategy of 'Three Warfare', namely employing media or public opinion, psychological warfare, and legal warfare seems to be finding some traction in politically active democracies, election oriented segments of population in India to settle their political scores.

Ladakh Standoff

The 15th round of Corps Commander level talks between India and China, ending with no concrete results, was not a surprise to anyone analysing Chinese activities, posture and signaling prior to the talks. The talks were preceded by the incidents of intrusions by Chinese troops in the Barahoti sector of Uttarakhand, the Tawang sector of Arunachal Pradesh, heavy concentration of troops and modern arsenal along LAC, exercises and building permanent structures in areas which China had encroached in mid-2020, vacation of which been the main agenda/purpose of the talks. It is amply evident that China is in no mood to concede anything and continues the talks for the optics of ongoing talkathon. Post disengagement of troops in Eastern Ladakh from North and South of Pangong Tso, some disengagement in Gogra, no disengagement has taken place in other areas to include Depsang plains, Patrolling Point 15 in Hot Spring area, Demchok, and no de-escalation, is a foregone conclusion, in view of activities mentioned earlier.

The Chinese intention to coerce India to resume business as usual, sidelining border/LAC issue and not insist on further pull back was refuted by the Indian Foreign Ministry by conveying that disengagement at all friction points leading to de-escalation, peace and tranquility on borders are pre-requisites to progressing smooth bilateral ties. This rightful Indian stance to get back to pre-April 2020 positions stands adversely affected by Chinese obnoxious allegation of India pushing for unreasonable and unrealistic demands, which is creating difficulties in negotiations, which indirectly conveys no more pulling back. Last year almost 80 percent of Chinese top leaders including President Xi Jinping have visited Tibet/Xinjiang. Massive infrastructure development in terms of airstrips, rail, road network to border towns like Nyngchi, accommodation and other activities are worth monitoring for India to work out its responses.

Aim and Strategies of China and India in Standoff so far

Chinese political aim was and continues to be China-centric Asia and forcing Indian subordination, a necessity to achieve it. This aim could not be achieved despite prolonged standoff in Ladakh so far, but will remain unchanged, even in future. Chinese strategic aim to control Eastern Ladakh was to provide depth to its National Highway G-219, Karakoram Pass, redraw Line of Actual Control[2] (LAC) as per its perception (1959-60) and negotiate border on its terms after that. China can claim to have partially achieved it, with a continued presence in extra kilometres in Depsang plains, Hot Spring, and Demchok areas, where disengagement hasn't occurred. Having developed its infrastructure in areas as per its perception of LAC, it aims to deny the same to India has not been so successful as India continues to develop its infrastructure at unprecedented speed to catch up. The Indian aim has been to get Chinese back to pre-standoff positions as of April 2020 in all friction points, not to concede unilateral change of LAC, and pursue talks towards its demarcation, hoping to lead to border resolution. With current disengagement, status quo stands achieved in areas north and south of Pangong Tso, albeit at the cost of losing the crucial leverage of giving up occupation of certain heights on Kailash range and north of Pangong Tso, prior to Chinese vacation of 'Other Areas'. Pursuing disengagement and de-escalation in remaining areas will be an uphill task due to shortage of leverages, given Chinese past track record and recent activities.

China marched in areas, where it was not supposed to be, junking all confidence-building measures (CBMs) as part of overall 'Incremental Encroachment Strategy', exploiting first mover advantage, making unfair use of Indian engagement in combating COVID-19 pandemic. China soon found itself handicapped by strong Indian response, resistance and resolve, with proactive actions resulting in newly created vulnerabilities to Maldo Garrison and its launch pad, South of Pangong Tso. Despite disengagement in Pangong Tso area, Chinese discomfort due to Indian dispositions in Sub Sector North including DBO, infrastructure development including DSDBO road, as a threat to crucial Tibet-Xinjiang-Pakistan connectivity remains. Except few proactive actions at tactical/operational level like Pangong Tso heights, Nathu La, and Doklam, by and large, the Indian national strategy against China has been reactive[3] in last seven decades.

A tale of Two Narratives to justify Partial Disengagement

It is a fact that none of the countries wanted a conflict; hence, both agreed for disengagement. Both countries justify their stance and disengagement process carried out so far favorable to them, although future of disengagement at remaining friction points is uncertain. The Chinese narrative to its population has been that it has got Indians down from heights north and south of Pangong Tso and ensured no Indian presence from Finger 4 to Finger 8 and Gogra, no patrolling by declaring it as buffer zone, while retaining its presence in Depsang plains, Hot Spring and Demchok areas. It can, therefore, claim to have edged forward 1959/60 claim line. The explainers of Chinese narrative will find it difficult to explain their gain by moving forward from Finger 8 to Finger 4 and then speedily withdrawing back to the same location, indicating weakness of PLA in high altitude area, besides making Maldo Garrison vulnerable and risking war, had Indians not obliged by pulling back from heights in Pangong Tso area.

The Indian narrative to its critiques is that it has successfully pushed the Chinese back to status quo ante positions as existed pre-standoff in Pangong Tso area, the stance which India maintained throughout. Amongst rest areas, like Hot Spring and Demchok, its work in progress to disengage and restore patrolling rights. Depsang is a legacy issue of decades, where patrolling points to limit Indo-Tibetan Border Police (ITBP)/Army patrols were designated to avoid confrontation. Willy-nilly, nearly two-thirds of Depsang Plateau remained outside the purview of our physical domination, which allowed PLA to establish intensive infrastructure and habitat in the area.[4] Depsang will, therefore, require separate discussion. India can also draw solace from the fact that, while it is being denied patrolling to the patrol points on Depsang Plateau East of the area Bottleneck inside the Raki Nallah, it has also denied PLA patrols movement West of Bottleneck, to Chinese claimed area close to Burtse. The explainers of Indian narrative will continue to find it difficult to explain why disengagement was not sequenced on 'first in and first out basis', meaning thereby that India should have vacated Kailash Range heights only after China had vacated the areas, where it advanced in Depsang plains, Gogra, Hot Spring and Demchok areas, since April 2020. It is reasonable to believe that it has left India at a disadvantage, due to shortage of worthwhile leverages. Notwithstanding the political debates over legacy of Depsang issue, it remains strategically important and a threat to Daulat Beg Oldi and Darbuk-Shyok-Daulat Beg Oldi Road; hence a concern for military professionals.

What can India do?

A serious push in capacity building and infrastructure build up along towards LAC to take on China challenge in recent past is encouraging. The responses must be in all domains, including contact and non-contact warfare. India needs a change in mindset from reactive to proactive, with additional offensive capability created to demonstrate capacity to encroach into sensitive areas of China, and inflict punitive cost, as China has assumed freedom to encroach anywhere, at will. The asymmetry in Comprehensive

National Power (CNP) between China and India is often cited as an excuse for muting proactive responses, but similar asymmetry exists between Pakistan and India, which doesn't hesitate in adopting unethical proactive proxy war against India under nuclear hangover. India also has nuclear triad, hence this excuse needs to be revisited. To express the intent, India could make 'One China Policy' conditional to One India Policy, as former and late Minister of External Affairs, Sushma Swaraj had mentioned in the past.

India needs to have part of its National Security Strategy (NSS), in open domain to steer capacity building to take on China's challenge in synergised manner. The classified part of NSS can be kept secret by all countries and should remain so. It is essential to prioritise the challenges and task required by various agencies to develop capacities avoiding different ministries working with different priorities, in silos. It's frustrating to see Public Interest Litigations (PILs) against broadening of strategic roads or railways dragging feet to construct strategic railway lines in Arunachal due to lack of commercial viability. Surely, part of NSS in open domain may improve sensitivity of all agencies to national security needs, once specified. India should also pass equivalent of Chinese Border Defence Law in some form, like strategic infrastructure along border to have different yardstick for speedy clearance by local, regional and central authorities to avoid incidents like the environment ministry obstructing many such constructions in the past. The reactive actions of India over several decades indicate 'Don't annoy China Approach", which has failed miserably as China has given no concession on displaying accommodation/goodwill so far. Not calling out Xinjiang or Hong Kong by India did not prevent China from dragging India to UN Security Council on Kashmir issue or not progressing CPEC on Indian sovereign territory. A change in mindset is required, from being reactive to being active with additional offensive capability to encroach into Chinese sensitive areas, in absence of which Chinese Western theatre Command has assumed no threat from India, with freedom to encroach anywhere, at will.

In light of trust deficit, recent activities along LAC, past track record of Chinese, un-demarcated LAC, and border between both countries, the ride ahead is unlikely to be smooth. With no de-escalation by Chinese, India is and will continue to be ready for all contingencies with similar deployment along LAC, in coming months/years. India needs to activate entire surveillance plan on high alert, to avoid any 'First mover advantage' to China like 2020. The Indian forces and the country has given a befitting reply to Chinese misadventure, and will do so each time, with added confidence and experience of 2020, including creating some new leverages, if needed.

Indian aim should be not to concede Chinese attempt to redraw LAC as LAC-2020. In light of no major breakthrough in 22nd round of China-India border talks, one may not expect any worthwhile development on delineation, delimitation for demarcation of LAC, which, is necessary to prevent repeated standoffs. India's strategic goal should be to insist on a formal delimitation and demarcation of the LAC, which is difficult but achievable, pending a permanent settlement of the Sino-Indian border issue. A temporary solution/side-lining main issue is recipe for the next standoff, leading to LOC-ization of LAC further. Chinese will like to keep border unsettled, till the time the political cost of not settling it becomes higher than doing so, for CCP, China.[5] Its efforts of bilateral border talks with Bhutan and Nepal including tri-junctions are to create further complications in the long-term resolution of borders. China will continue to try encroaching Bhutanese land to create more space in Chumbi Valley, to threaten the Siliguri Corridor.

India must be prepared for 'Two Front War' as a worst case scenario, and continue capacity building in all domains, including maritime arena, where Chinese vulnerable sea lines of communications can be threatened. Besides ongoing infrastructure development along borders, in response to Chinese build-up of hundreds of new well off villages to incrementally change the ground position, it is recommended that States/UT along LAC should allot concessional land to security forces[6] and families hailing from that area (on son of soil concept), ready to settle in villages so constructed, along own perception of LAC. This will improve inclusive growth, integration, besides proof of our claims on the border, to ward off 'Chinese Strategy of Incremental Encroachment'. The best way to fight a two front war is to convince both adversaries that we can fight it, not by words alone, but backed by appropriate capacity building and intent to use all levers of power.

In response to economic and digital encroachment, India must increasingly draw out a negative import list of all products imported from China, which have been/can be manufactured in India and increasingly ban their imports, as is being done to improve self-reliance in defence manufacturing. It may sound unpleasant to few profit making importers, but will reduce our dependencies and concerns of economic coercion to great extent in long term. It's absurd to notice India's trade surplus with China growing beyond its defence budget during standoff period.

Strategic partnerships with like-minded democracies and collective naval posturing with like-minded democracies to create multi-front situation for China in Indo-Pacific is essential to check Chinese expansionism challenging global order and threatening global commons with steps like China centric Coast Guard Law and Maritime Traffic Safety Law.[7] India is rightly building series of strategic partnerships with the USA and other China-wary Asian countries mitigate continuing Chinese military assistance and activity around India. There is a need for alternative supply chain, trade and technological eco system, independent of China for which some initial steps taken by Quad countries need to be pursued. Alternate infrastructure architecture in the form of B3W, Blue Dot Network and Friendship Highways are essential to save fragile economies getting into debt trap of China through BRI. The announcement of Indo-Pacific Economic Forum (IPEF) is a welcome step in this direction. Collective responses against cyber, space, biological threats and nuclear expansion need to be worked out.

India needs to develop its strategic culture with professional strategists, as diplomacy driven patch ups and talkathon have not worked so far. The overall strategic approach has to be proactive at all levels in all dimensions of warfare. The overall strategic approach has to be proactive at tactical, operational as well as strategic level.

Endnotes

1   Shuxian Luo (2021), "China's land border law: A preliminary assessment", URL: https://www.brookings.edu/blog/order-from-chaos/2021/11/04/chinas-land-border-law-a-preliminary-assessment/

2   Maj Gen Shashi Asthana (2020), "Decoding Chinese strategic intent in prolonged standoff at LAC", URL: https://www.wionews.com/opinions-blogs/decoding-chinese-strategic-intent-in-prolonged-standoff-at-lac-328945

3   Maj Gen Shashi Asthana (2021), "Revisiting Mountain Strike Corps Amidst Ladakh Standoff", URL: http://www.indiandefencereview.com/news/revisiting-mountain-strike-corps-amidst-ladakh-standoff/

4   Lt Gen (Dr) Rakesh Sharma (Retd.) (2021), "Agreement on Disengagement at LAC: A Short, Positive Step Forward...", URL: https://www.vifindia.org/article/2021/february/15/agreement-on-disengagement-on-lac-a-short-positive-step-forward

5   Maj Gen Shashi Asthana (2021), "LAC disengagement: Difficult to trust China", URL: https://www.sundayguardianlive.com/opinion/lac-disengagement-difficult-trust-china?fbclid=IwAR3OQ0K7mnOSiU4JZpKCjLh4zZl9k2kFTjEkjHOdIJPDXJFjgqMQ89Flk0U

6   Maj Gen Shashi Asthana (2021), "China-India Standoff at LAC: Extrapolating possibilities in 2021", URL: https://government.economictimes.indiatimes.com/news/defence/china-india-standoff-at-lac-extrapolating-possibilities-in-2021/80927572

7   Maritime Traffic Safety Law of the People's Republic of China, 2021, URL: http://www.npc.gov.cn/npc/c30834/202104/9dfede4d82aa4fc1ae8ca22e987e025b.shtml

Chapter 3

India's Tibet-China Policy: Tectonic Shift From Nehru To Modi

Vijay Kranti

Introduction

India and Tibet today share about 4000 km long borders along the entire length of Himalayas. While it is one of the longest 'unsettled' and tense borders between two countries across the world today, it had the distinction of being one of the most peaceful international borders over centuries until People's Republic of China (PRC) forcibly occupied Tibet in 1951. This may sound funny but PRC's People Liberation Army (PLA) and its communist masters declared this act as 'peaceful liberation' of Tibet and the 'return' of Tibet to the fold of 'Great Motherland'. This act of Mao Zedong, the revolutionary dictator of PRC, changed the centuries old 'India-Tibet border' into 'India-China border' overnight. Before the Younghusband military expedition of the British ruled India invaded Tibet in 1903-04 and the following Shimla-Treaty between British India, Tibet and China was signed in 1914 in India's Himalayan town of Shimla, the relations between India and Tibet were more defined as ones between two cultural entities than two political nation-states since time immemorial. From time immemorial until 1951, this border was known as the India-Tibet border. Not even Chinese historians ever mentioned it as 'India-China' border.

India and Tibet had been maintaining all formal border relations like controlling the passages, maintenance of peace, postal relations and border trade through representatives of Indian and Tibetan governments. At no stage in history any Chinese official ever played any role along any section on this 4000 km long border. Interestingly, China's attempts to extend its borders up to South Asia and India had already started in 1949. Soon after coming to power the Communist rulers of the newly found PRC invaded and occupied erstwhile 'Republic of East Turkistan'. In their hurry to give it a Chinese name they rechristened the RET with a new Chinese name 'Xinjiang' which, literally means 'New Frontier'. China's sudden occupation of East Turkistan brought it face to face for the first time in history along the Ladakh and Gilgit-Baltistan regions that are legally part of Indian territory. Later, after occupying Tibet in 1951, this 4000 and odd km long border line joining the two ends of India-China (nee 'India-Tibet') border runs along Himachal Pradesh (India), Nepal, Sikkim (India), Bhutan and Arunachal Pradesh and remains unmarked and unsettled till this day. Since then India's Tibet policy has been reflected mainly through its policy towards China.

India's Historic Tibet Policy

Though India gained her independence on 15th August, 1947, yet the world had first glimpse of its independent foreign policy five months in advance when Pandit Jawahar Lal Nehru, the provisional head of the government of India organized 'Asian Relations Conference' in March-April same year in New Delhi.

Tibet and China participated in this conference as two different nations and the Tibetan delegates as well as Tibetan flag adored the main dais along with China's. Earlier in January 1946 Nehru had categorically mentioned Tibet as an independent nation in his invitation to Mahatma Gandhi as well as in his welcome speech. In his speech he said, *".... We welcome you delegates and representatives from China, that great country to which Asia owes so much and from which so much is expected; from Egypt and the Arab countries ... from Iran .... from Indonesia and Indo-China... from Turkey.... from Korea and Mongolia, Siam, Malaya and the Philippines; from the Soviet Republics of Asia.... from our neighbours Afghanistan, Tibet, Nepal, Bhutan, Burma and Ceylon to whom we look especially for co-operation and close and friendly intercourse...*(J L Nehru's Speech at Asian Relations Conference, 1947)"[1]

When Nehru became first Prime Minister of free India, his Foreign Office wrote to the Tibetan government: *"...The Government of India would be glad to have an assurance that it is the intention of the Tibetan government to continue relations on the existing basis until new arrangements are reached that either party may wish to take up. This is the procedure adopted by all other countries with which India has inherited treaty relations from His Majesty' Government...* (Notes, Memoranda and Letters Exchanged and Agreements Signed by the Governments of India and China, 1959)."[2]

This assertion of Nehru government about evolving and carrying forward relations with Tibet on equal footing was natural because India was among that small group of three countries, namely Nepal, China and British India, which had formal relations with the Tibetan government and had been maintaining their official ambassadorial missions in Lhasa since decades. India also ran its two permanent business and commerce consulate offices in Tibet at Yatung and Gyantse along with a seasonal consulate office in Gartok. India was the only country which had rights to maintain an army unit and telegraph system in Tibet. The Indian mission in Lhasa functioned until 1952 when it was downgraded by Pt. Nehru's government to the 'Consulate General' level on insistence of his 'friend' Chinese Prime Minister Chou En Lai.

This presence of India in Tibet had its source in the historic' Lhasa Convention' of September-1904[3] which was signed between British India and the government of Tibet when the 13th Dalai Lama was its ruler (Convention between Great Britain and Tibet, 1904). It was signed following the successful completion of 'Younghusband Expedition' of the British government of India to Lhasa.

Yet another major proof of India's recognition of Tibet as a sovereign country, especially in relations with India, lies in the historic 'McMahon Line' which has come to stay as the boundary line between erstwhile Indian State of Assam in the South and Tibet in the North. The contours of this line were agreed in the famous 'Shimla Convention'[4] of Oct 1913-July 1914 in which British India, Tibet and China participated as three different countries (Legal Materials on Tibet: Convention Between Great Britain, China, and Tibet, Simla, 1914). Interestingly, this treaty was signed only between British India and Tibet because China refused to sign it on the ground that it did not agree with the Tibetan government representatives on some issues related to boundary between Tibet and China.

In his book 'Tibet and its History' *(Oxford University Press, 1961)*, Hugh E. Richardson, who worked as the last Consul General of British India in Lhasa from 1936 till 1949 as India's representative, states: *"The Government of Lhasa which I dealt was beyond question in complete control of its own affairs dealing directly with the Government of India in such matters as frontier disputes, trade questions, supply of arms and ammunition and so on. There was no Chinese participation whatsoever in such matters and no reference to them, nor were they informed. In all practical matters the Tibetan were independent...."* (Richardson, 1961)."5

Lord Curzon, the Viceroy of India had already defined Tibet's status in his note of January 8, 1903 to the Secretary of State in charge of Indian affairs in London. Recommending a military expedition to Lhasa (that fructified as the 'Younghusband Mission') he wrote, *"We regard the so-called suzerainty of China over Tibet as a constitutional fiction, a political affectation which has been maintained because of its convenience to both parties... As a matter of fact, the two Chinese (the Manchu Ambans) at Lhasa are there not as Viceroys, but as ambassadors."* (British Expedition to Tibet, Wikipedia)."6

All these historic facts show that until before Tibet was invaded and occupied by the Communist regime of People's Republic of China (PRC), Indian government's policies were based on this unambiguous assumption that Tibet was an independent country and that China had no role in India-Tibet relations.

The Nehru Factor and Tibet

Looking back now, it can be said that it was the dramatic victory of Chinese Communist Party's bloody revolution under the leadership of Chairman Mao Tse Tung (now 'Mao Zedong') over Nationalist government of Kuomintang in China had an overwhelming impact on Prime Minister Nehru. A socialist Nehru visualized the dream of a new Asia, based on India-China friendship, where he would be acknowledged as a 'world statesman'. Later developments in India-China relations show that in his enthusiasm to be seen in good books of Mao and Chou, Nehru would not only overturn his own publicly proclaimed views on Tibet, but would also refuse to listen to any voice of reason on China's aggression against Tibet from anyone else in his own government or other Indian leaders. For example, on 1st January 1950 when Mao made the historic announcement regarding 'liberation' of Tibet and Tibetans as a 'basic task' for the PLA,

Nehru turned a blind eye to it despite strong opposition and apprehensions expressed by other Indian leaders. Rather, on 21st August, 1950 when Chinese government made public its intentions of solving the problem of Tibet by 'peaceful and friendly' measures and to "stabilize the China-India borders", Nehru government formally expressed its appreciation for the 'peaceful' intensions of PRC about their proposed actions in Tibet. It did not even point out to China that it was 'India-Tibet' border what China was referring to as 'China-India' border. Nehru believed that any military action by China in Tibet would have harmful effects on India's advocacy for PRC's entry into the UN. New Delhi had already rebuffed Tibetan government's requests for help or intervention.

China attacked eastern parts of Tibet on 7th October 1950. Over 40,000 soldiers of PLA invaded and occupied Chamdo, the provincial capital of Tibet's Kham province without much resistance from Tibetan side. For all practical purpose, Tibet had lost the game to a bully Mao and his PLA. When Tibet sent appeal for help to New Delhi, the Nehru government refused to intervene. It was now left to the 15-year-old Dalai Lama, the theocratic teenager king of Tibet to surrender or face blood bath at the hands of ruthless communist forces of China.

Sardar Patel on Tibet

Sardar Vallabhbhai Patel, the Deputy Prime Minister and Home Minister of India, the next tallest Indian leader in Nehru's government, summed up the gravity of Chinese attack on Tibet in his letter to Nehru on 7th November, 1950. It was a long letter but some of his observations (as attached in Appendix I), far sightedness and vision surprise political observers even today:

> "...... The final action of the Chinese, in my judgment, is little short of perfidy. The tragedy of it is that the Tibetans put faith in us; they choose to be guided by us; and we have been unable to get them out of the meshes of Chinese diplomacy or Chinese malevolence......... we have to consider what new situation now faces us as a result of the disappearance of Tibet, as we knew it, and the expansion of China almost up to our gates. Throughout history we have seldom been worried about our north-east frontier. The Himalayas have been regarded as an impenetrable barrier against any threat from the north. We had friendly Tibet which gave us no trouble............. We can, therefore,

safely assume that very soon they (Chinese government) will disown all the stipulations which Tibet has entered into with us in the past. That throws into the melting pot all frontier and commercial settlements with Tibet on which we have been functioning and acting during the last half a century. (Sardar Vallabhbhai Patel's Letter to Pt Jawahar Lal Nehru, 1950). [7]

Records show that Nehru refused to even acknowledge this letter's receipt. Luckily for Nehru, the only other voice, that of Mahatma Gandhi, who could have challenged his stubborn and arrogant attitude on a delicate and serious issues like occupation of Tibet, had already been silenced by the bullets of a rogue gunman in early days of 1948. As the luck would have it, Sardar Patel too was soon incapacitated by tuberculosis and died soon after, leaving Nehru completely free to take decisions on Tibet and China. Since India was going to be the most affected third country by Chinese plans of taking over Tibet, New Delhi was left with only two choices - either to stand up for Tibet or turn a blind eye to the turning of Indo-Tibetan border into Indo-Chinese one. Nehru chose the second. Later when Lhasa government approached India and other countries for help, Nehru appeared so much influenced by Chinese Premier Chou En Lai's assurances of good conduct, respect for Tibet's autonomy, non-interference in Tibetan culture and development of Tibet that he discouraged world powers like Britain and USA from taking any action against China. India even dissuaded United Nations from taking up El Salvador's demand to discuss Tibet in the UN in November 1950. Even when China manipulated the Tibetan government to sign a much-touted '17-Point Agreement' on 23rd May 1951 for the 'Peaceful Liberation of Tibet' and its assimilation into China, Nehru refused to oppose this Chinese move.

The Panchsheel Blunder

Chou's magic spell on Nehru finally lead to the historic "Panchsheel Agreement" between India and China in 1954 in which the government of India not only formally acknowledged Tibet as an 'Autonomous Region of China', it also forfeited all the privileges like maintaining its mission and three Consulate offices which India enjoyed historically in Tibet. In 1956 when Dalai Lama visited India to take part in 2500 year celebrations of Lord Buddha's enlightenment, he expressed his desire to seek asylum in India. But Nehru practically scolded him and sent him back with the advice to cooperate with the Chinese. It was only following the ruthless massacre of over 80,000 Tibetans by the Chinese Army in 1959 in Tibet that India granted asylum to Dalai Lama after his daring escape across the Himalayas to India. But Nehru's support to China on Tibet continued unabated.

India in the United Nations

In later years when United Nations General Assembly passed two resolutions against China for human rights violations inside Tibet in 1959 and 1961, Nehru's India abstained in the voting. But India was shoved out of its slumber and Beijing's magic spell only in 1962 when China used occupied Tibet as a launch pad to attack India and gave her a humiliating military defeat. In 1965 when same resolution, condemning China for human rights denials in Tibet, was put to vote in the UN, India voted in its favour. But it was already too late (UN General Assembly Resolution 2079).[8]. This was the first, and seemingly the last time, so far, when India formally registered its opposition to China's occupation of Tibet or its colonial deeds therein. This development once again underlined that instead of practicing an independent Tibet policy, New Delhi governments' decisions about Tibet have always been limited only to convenient options or obvious corollaries of its immediate relations with China.

Joining Hands with Pakistan

The monumental increase in China's military and economic power and its grip over Tibet over the years has successively reduced India's choices on Tibet. Thanks to New Delhi's blind faith in Chinese leaders and near total indifference towards its border regions in early 1950s, China quietly usurped Aksai Chin region, a strategically located 37,244 sq km region of India's Ladakh and merged it with the Hotan region of Xinjiang. Following 1962 war with India, the Chinese government found a willing partner in Pakistan who happily transferred another strategically located Shaksgam Valley (area 6993 sq km) from its occupied part of India's Ladakh to China in 1963. Both of these regions have given a big strategic boost to China in its western most region. It first helped China in connecting Tibet with Xinjiang through Karakoram Highway and later in developing a direct modern transportation access to the Arabian Sea through China Pakistan Economic Project (CPEC) and constructing a deep sea naval base in the Arabian Sea at Gwadar in the Baluchistan province of Pakistan. This port has not only fortified Pakistani Naval power vis-à-vis India in the Arabian

Sea, it has also provided a new strategic foothold to China on its Western front which was otherwise geographically impossible since centuries. Although a substantial part of the CPEC has been constructed on areas of Pakistan occupied Jammu and Kashmir (POK) which India claims as its own, yet the Indian government could not do anything in this matter accept sitting as a helpless spectator.

India: A Reluctant Fighter

Events following the 1962 India-China war show that while China had taken full advantage of its occupation and its strong military infrastructure in Tibet to dominate India, the latter had emerged only as a victim of its own halfhearted approach on the issue of Tibet. Rather than confronting China on its indefensible human rights record in Tibet; or as a direct next door victim of China's colonial occupation of Tibet; or using the presence of Dalai Lama and his international stature to its advantage, New Delhi could never go beyond playing the role of an apologetic and reluctant fighter. For example, it offered asylum to Dalai Lama only as the 'supreme spiritual leader' of Tibetans but not as the 'exiled ruler' of an occupied country. It allows Dalai Lama to run his establishment through an elected Parliament in Dharamshala only as the 'Central Tibetan Administration', and not as 'Government in Exile' of Tibet. This reluctant Indian support to Tibet found its best expression during the Bangladesh liberation war in 1971. The Tibetan guerrillas, belonging to the Special Frontier Force (SFF) of Indian Army which worked directly under the command of late Prime Minister Indira Gandhi's Cabinet Secretariat, played a decisive role in liberating the Tripura-Chittagong parts of erstwhile East Pakistan. But the Government of India has yet to officially acknowledge this contribution of Tibetans in India's historic military victory over Pakistan for creating an independent Bangladesh.

Mira Sinha Bhattacharjea Syndrome

A unique feature of India's foreign policy, especially on China and Tibet, is that it has been perpetually guided or run by the leftist (read 'Marxist') lobby among Indian policy experts, think-tanks, intellectuals and Foreign Ministry bureaucrats influenced by them. Until Narendra Modi took over as Prime Minister of India in 2014, a dominant section among 'China experts' and 'Sinologists' in the power circles, universities of India and even in the MEA itself have been suffering from what this author terms as 'Mira

Sinha Bhattacharjea Syndrome'. Mira was the famous lady Indian diplomat and a celebrated leftist, who left the coveted Indian Foreign Service to teach Sinology in Delhi University and gave direction to India's China policy through think tanks like Institute of Chinese Studies (ICS). Under her intellectual stewardship a vast majority of 'China Experts' of India have won the distinction of framing India's typical approach towards China which, in most cases, has been far more subservient to China's sensitivities and their national interests than those of India.

The best example of this 'Syndrome' came in 2003 when BJP leader Atal Bihari Vajpayee, one of the most vocal and active supporters of Tibetan freedom as an opposition leader, visited Beijing as India's Prime Minister. Overwhelmed by the counsel of his conventional 'China Experts', he signed the India-China agreement of peace and tranquility in which India officially accepted "Tibet Autonomous Region as a part of the territory of People's Republic of China." (India-China Joint Declaration, 2003). [9] His office later claimed that this change was in bargain for China's recognition for Sikkim as a part of India. But Beijing soon made it clear that its stand on Sikkim remained same. Rather, in the following years China started claiming India's Arunachal Pradesh as 'South Tibet'.

Modi's Shift in Tibet-China Policy?

However, since May 2014, India's Narendra Modi government has taken quite a few steps which indicate towards a qualitative shift in India's approach towards China. Tibet supporters can now hope that India might evolve an independent Tibet policy that is less driven by its reactions to Beijing's actions on India and more on India's own long term national interests vis-à-vis Tibet as its immediate neighbor. Interestingly, there have been quite a few developments since Mr. Modi took charge as Indian Prime Minister in 2014 which indicate that the Government of India is slowly coming out of a reactive China policy to a proactive one. For example, on 26th May 2014 when Mr. Modi took oath of his office as Prime Minister of India first time in New Delhi, all heads of State from India's neighborhood except China's Xi Jinping were invited to the glittering ceremony in Rashtrapati Bhawan, the President House of India. Interestingly, Dr. Lobsang Sangay, the elected 'Sikyong' (then 'Prime Minister' of Tibetan government in exile, now re-designated as the 'President') was seen sitting in the section, reserved for Heads of State. Later when Modi chose countries like Bhutan, Brazil and

Nepal for his initial foreign visits, a sulking Beijing had to virtually cajole New Delhi for President Xi Jinping's visit to India which finally happened in September that year.

But as always, China played its old game of needling India a couple of days before the start of this visit by pushing a column of Chinese PLA into the Indian territory of Ladakh claiming that the area belonged to China. It has been a common practice of Beijing to do something irritating and aggressive like this on the eve of a senior Indian leader's visit to China or a Chinese leader visiting India with an aim to bully and demoralize Indian leaders in order to dominate the discussions. Many times the government agencies of India would even embargo the Indian media on publishing news of such Chinese incursions. But this time the process went reverse. Indian media went crazy in highlighting this Chinese military aggression. Knowledgeable sources later revealed that President Xi was given a clear choice of pulling back the PLA soldiers to Tibet side by the same night or be ready to wind up his visit premature next morning in Gujarat, the home state of Modi. To the surprise of Indian media and people, PLA soldiers withdrew same night. In April 2016, despite strong opposition from Beijing, Modi government in New Delhi permitted Dalai Lama's CTA in Dharamsala to go ahead with its 4-day 'international' conference of representatives of Tibet, 'Southern Mongolia', 'East Turkistan' (Xinjiang), Falun Gong and Chinese Democracy movement from across the globe who have been fighting against Chinese hegemony for their respective freedom movements of human rights causes (India Today, 2016).[10] In past 60 years no Indian government would have even thought of entertaining such an idea.

India after Doklam and Galwan

But the most significant event of the Modi-era, which reflects a qualitative changes in New Delhi's approach towards China, is the Doklam and Galwan incidents. Doklam episode took place between June and August of 2017 at the Tibet-Bhutan- India tri-junction. This 73 day long high pitched drama surprised the world and shocked the communist rulers of Beijing when Indian Armymen physically stood up to PLA troops to stop them from constructing a road into the Bhutanese territory and forced the Chinese government to pull back (India Today, 2018)[11]. During the bloody clash with Chinese soldiers in June 2020, Indian Army soldiers showed exemplary courage and matched China's aggression leaving many Chinese soldiers dead and wounded.

There are many other examples which indicate that things are changing in New Delhi on India's Tibet and China policy. In March 2017 New Delhi not only permitted the Dalai Lama to visit Arunachal Pradesh despite strong protests and warnings from Beijing, the State government even provided all the security and hospitality to him (Press Trust of India, 2017). [12] Modi government has also undertaken a new initiative of developing a network of roads along its Himalayan borders with Tibet, an initiative consistently and deliberately avoided by previous Congress governments who would chose to play cool rather than take China head on matters of defence preparedness along Tibetan borders. One of the reasons for frequent border-standoffs between India and China in recent years is better road connectivity on Indian side of border with China. Modi government's latest step of establishing a stand-alone integrated defence system on its North Eastern borders along Arunachal Pradesh indicates its seriousness towards attending to nation's popular threat perception from China. Indian Army's Northern Command holds an exceptionally high level military exercise in 'Super High Altitudes' near Tibetan border in Eastern Ladakh. Comprising of a specially raised elite force named "Fire and Fury Corps" it is considered as the most modern mechanized forces with force multipliers integrating high technology platforms, established especially for the Himalayan borders with China and Pakistan. "This command will excel in combat, should conflict be forced upon us", said Lt Gen Ranbir Singh, Chief of Indian Army's Northern Command who personally supervised the exercise in 2019 (*The New Indian Express*, 2019). [13]

Interestingly, when Prsident Xi Jinping met PM Modi for 2nd informal summit in October 2019 in Chennai, the Indian Army's Mountain Strike Corps conducted a major exercise 'Him Vijay' (meaning Snow Victory) in far eastern states of Arunachal Pradesh and Assam, bordering Tibet, with its newly created integrated Battle Groups involving 15 thousand troops (The Economic Times, 2019).[14] This was an unprecedented posture adopted by any New Delhi government vis-à-vis China in past 0ver 70 years. More so on the eve of a Chinese Presidential visit. New Delhi's new approach towards China has had a major expression at international levels in May 2017 when it not only opposed Xi Jinping's idea of 'Belt and Road Initiative (BRI)' but also boycotted the international BRI conference in Beijing. Over the period, India has taken its own initiative of developing a shared network of new roads with many neighbor countries like Bangladesh, Myanmar and other countries in South East Asia. Now that a hawkish Xi Jinping has successfully rooted himself more strongly in the Chinese system and has got the BRI included in the Constitution of CPC during 19th Congress in Beijing, the shape of India's Tibet-China policy has become more challenging for India and more interesting for the rest of world. Modi government's special focus on improving its defence capabilities, developing relations and fortifying strategic cooperation with Eastern countries and active participation in forums with member countries like USA, Japan, Australia, Vietnam etc who are keen to take Chinese hegemony head on, indicates that new India of Modi is redefining its relations with China. One can now expect a fresh revaluation of India's approach towards Tibet in due course too.

Endnotes

1   J L Nehru's Speech at Asian Relations Conferences. (1947). Accessed September 28, 2019, https://sites.google.com/site/legalmaterialsontibet/home/asian-relations-conference

2   Notes, Memoranda and Letters Exchanged and Agreements Signed by the Governments of India and China, Vol.2, 1959, P-39.

3   Convention between Great Britain and Tibet - Signed at Lhasa, September 7, 1904,Document-3. The Question of Tibet and the Rule of Law. .*International Commission of Jurists Geneva*, 1959. Accessed October 1, 2019, http://www.icj.org/wp-content/uploads/1959/01/Tibet-rule-of-law-report-1959-eng.pdf

4   Legal Materials on Tibet : Convention Between Great Britain, China, and Tibet, Simla. (1914). [400]. *Attached to the Anglo-Tibetan Declaration of 3 July 1914.* Accessed October 2, 2019, http://www.tibetjustice.org/materials/treaties/treaties16.html

5   Hugh E. Richardson. (1961). *Tibet and its History*. Oxford University Press.

6   British Expedition to Tibet (Wikipedia). Accessed September 25, 2019, https://en.wikipedia.org/wiki/British_expedition_to_Tibet

7   Full text of Sardar Vallabhbhai Patel's Letter to Pt Jawahar Lal Nehru. (1950). Accessed September 27, 2019, http://www.friendsoftibet.org/main/sardar.html

8   UN General Assembly Resolution 2079.(1965). Accessed October 1, 2019, https://www.tibetpolicy.eu/un-general-assembly-resolution-2079-xx-of-1965/

9   India-China Joint Declaration. (2003). *Times of India*, June 24, Accessed October 3, 2019, "https://timesofindia.indiatimes.com/Full-text-of-India-China-joint-Declaration/articleshow/41346.cms

10   India Today. (2016). *China fumes as India issues visa to Uyghur separatist.* April 22, Accessed October 5, https://www.indiatoday.in/mail-today/story/china-blames-india-for-hosting-its-terrorist-319260-2016-04-22

11   India Today. (2018).*Where is Doklam and why it is important for India?.* March 27.Accessed October 5, https://www.indiatoday.in/education-today/gk-current-affairs/story/where-doklam-why-important-india-china-bhutan-1198730-2018-03-27

12   Press Trust of India. (2017). As Dalai Lama visits Arunachal Pradesh, China vows to take 'necessary measures. *The Hindu*, April 5, Accessed October 5,

https://www.thehindu.com/news/national/china-vows-necessary-measure-after-dalai-lama-visits-arunachal-pradesh/article17824312.ece

13   The New Indian Express.   (2019). *Army's Northern Command Chief presides over military exercise in Eastern Ladakh.* September 18, Accessed October   6.http://www.newindianexpress.com/nation/2019/sep/18/armys-northern-command-chief-presides-over-military-exercise-in-eastern-ladakh-2035406.html

14   The Economic Times (2019). *India to deploy latest American weapon systems for Ex-Him Vijay along China border.* September 13, Accessed October 8,   https://economictimes.indiatimes.com/news/defence/india-to-deploy-latest-american-weapon-systems-for-ex-himvijay-along-china-border/articleshow/71108992.cms

Section II

Science, Technology and Military Modernisation

Chapter 4

India's Defence Policy in Recent Years: A World of Opportunities

Rahul Bhonsle

Introduction: Defence Policy-Making Process in India

As a parliamentary democracy, policy-making in India is a collective function. In the case of defence policy, the Cabinet Committee on Security (CCS) is the final arbiter after distillation at multiple executive and advisory levels from the armed forces, the National Security Council and numerous public and private think tanks that dot the national panorama. While the Prime Minister chairs the CCS, the defence, external affairs, home and finance ministers are members. In the past decade, the world has seen the rise of strong leaders; some may even say authoritarian leaders, whether former US President Donald Trump, Vladimir Putin in Russia or Xi Jinping in China. It is not surprising that some analysts categorise Narendra Modi in the same genre though, "decisive," may be a more appropriate adjective to describe his style. This is evident on the consultative process for major action-oriented decisions that have been taken by Prime Minister Modi within three months of his second tenure. These include the "surgical strikes" land and air undertaken in 2016 and 2019[1] or repealing provisions of Article 370 or special status to Jammu and Kashmir in August 2019.

An important deduction drawn is that while options or surgical strikes or revocation of Article 370 may have been examined earlier, in fact these were extensively debated in the past particularly after the 2008 Mumbai 26/11 terror attack, but it was decisive leadership that was provided by

PM Modi in undertaking these and then seeing through implementation. For the future, this clearly informs us that decisions will be guided by a well-considered policy to ensure attainment of core national interests. Discerning the defence policy of a government in India is not an easy task given that there is no written document that outlines a doctrine or strategy that is guiding defence planners and the armed forces. In the absence of the same, reliance has to be placed on a large number of primary source documents such as official speeches of principal leaders - the Prime Minister, Defence Minister, doctrines published by the armed forces, party election manifestos and so on. Based on a review of these sources, a clearer perception does emerge on the trajectory of India's defence policy in recent years which has been covered in succeeding paragraphs.

Drivers of India's Defence Policy

Policies are driven by core values, beliefs and thought processes of principal decision-makers. As an emerging power, India's ambition of shaping the global agenda in the 21st century has a major security component particularly in the regional environment that is obtained in the Indian sub-continent and increasingly in the Indo-Pacific. Use of force, however, will remain an exception. Fulfilment of aspiration will be by promoting and creating a peaceful environment rather than raw exercise of power. Speaking at an event in New Delhi on the occasion of Buddha Purnima Prime Minister in May 2018, Prime Minister Narendra Modi asserted, "India has never been an aggressor, in history".[2] The Indian Army's Land Warfare Doctrine published in 2018 states that the "primary approach of India is to resolve disputes in an amicable manner, with national objectives being achieved through a mix of politico-diplomatic initiatives". On the other hand, the armed forces will remain vigilant and ready to prosecute military operations in a multi-front scenario in all dimensions, to achieve the politico-military objectives. Thus, war prevention through deterrence remains the core objective at the national level to achieve which the armed forces will be the main instrument of the state externally.[3]

Underlying that while India's foreign and defence policy will continue to be generally conciliatory, where national interest so demands aggressive action is not ruled out. This is amply evident from the two surgical strikes that were launched in 2016 and 2019 where Prime Minister Modi and his national security team determined that a punitive action was necessary to establish counter terror deterrence against Pakistan. These actions were taken after diplomatic outreach failed including a personal visit by the Prime Minister for a short halt in Lahore in December 2015. Ironically, this initiative to Pakistan was followed by the terrorist attack on the Pathankot air base almost within a week on 2nd January 2016 and culminated in another major strike in Uri in September 2016. This convinced the Government of India for a decisive cross border lesson to be taught to the adversary which was delivered successfully. India had also stood up to China's constant border incursions and Indian military had a 73-day long border standoff with the People's Liberation Army at Doklam in 2017.

Strategic Environment

A review of the strategic environment faced by India has been carried out from time to time in various forums which will guide the defence policy. In a world that is undergoing rapid disruptive changes, there is a shift in the international order that is ongoing at a pace that was never seen before as per the Ministry of Defence Annual Report 2018-19.[4] India plans to develop appropriate responses, to shape the international environment conducive to India's development and security as per the Annual Report. The flux includes "complex and increasingly unpredictable interplay of regional and global developments," which are expected to pose challenge to retain the core principles of India's foreign policy i.e. strategic autonomy. Threats envisaged are not just conventional but increasingly sub conventional such as terrorism and radicalisation growing laterally and horizontally requiring sustained commitment of diplomacy and force if required to make the nation free from the menace of terror. Proliferation of Weapons of Mass Destruction (WMD) including delivery systems remains a major challenge and will not go away soon which is evident with the revocation of the Intermediate Range Nuclear Forces or INF (Intermediate range nuclear force) Treaty in August 2019 by the United States (US) and Russia this may result in the US deploying these categories of weapons in the Indo-Pacific. Correspondingly, response from China could be anticipated, in the context of India's nuclear dilemma can be anticipated. Thus, a complex strategic environment with multi-dimensional threats in a rapidly transforming World is evident. In the wake of Russia-Ukraine crisis that began on February 24, 2022, there has been a lot of spotlight on India's defence relationship with Russia. Western countries have sought to put pressure on India to scale down its military cooperation with Russia.

However, this may not happen anytime soon although India has been already diversifying sources of its arms imports which has reduced share of Russia in its defence market in the last decade. This crisis has also forced the government of India to augment its efforts towards defence indigenisation.

Strategic Security Direction

Given the lack of a written document on defence and security, reliance to identify the same will have to be placed on the most recent policy speeches. The Vice President of India, M. Venkaiah Naidu while delivering a Lecture at the National Defence College on the theme "India's Strategic Culture, National Core Values, Interests and Objectives," on 15 October 2018, outlined the strategic security direction to include following components:

(a) Maintaining a deterrent capability to safeguard National Interests.

(b) Ensuring security of national territory, maritime region, including the trade routes, air space and cyber space.

(c) Maintaining a secure internal environment to guard against threats for the unity and development.

(d) Strengthening and Expanding "Constructive Engagement" with Nations to promote regional and global peace as also international stability.[5]

Strategic Including Nuclear Deterrence

Strengthening the nuclear triad will remain the core focus to ensure strategic deterrence not just in the nuclear but also in space and cyber domains as has been demonstrated by the ASAT (Anti Satellite) tests carried out in March 2019.[6] Taking a cue from its earlier tenure where Modi government sanctioned operational deployment of the Strategic Strike Nuclear Submarine (SSBN) INS Arihant, on a deterrence patrol thus establishing the country's survivable nuclear triad in 2018. The seventh test of the AGNI V [third during 2018] was also carried out achieving two key milestones in the strategic missile development programmes. Agni V, the long-range surface-to-surface Nuclear Capable Ballistic missile is now being handled with the Strategic Forces Command (SFC), however, there is no clarity of operational induction of the strategic system. On 27 March 2019, Defense Research and Development Organization (DRDO) successfully conducted an Anti-Satellite (A-SAT) missile test 'Mission

Shakti' from the Dr. APJ Abdul Kalam Island in Odisha by successfully engaging an Indian orbiting target satellite in Low Earth Orbit (LEO) in a 'Hit to Kill' mode. This was seen as a signal to potential adversaries of strike capability in the space domain.

Multi Front Capability, Multi Domain capability is the buzzword. In the multi front scenario it is envisaged that two fronts may have to be addresses such as Pakistan and China. For this purpose, deterrence on one front and operations on the other will ensure optimal capability utilisation. Multi-Dimensional nature of conflicts was also emphasised at the Kargil Vijay Diwas function in Delhi in July 2019, Prime Minister had outlined that conflicts have reached space, and the cyber world thus multi domain capability building has been identified as a core area for modernisation of armed forces in the future.

The No First Use (NFU) clause in the nuclear doctrine is unlikely to change even though there has been much debate over the past few years. Members of the strategic community in Delhi have indicated from time to time that this has served India well and a review is not necessary even though Pakistan has developed battlefield tactical nuclear rockets.[7]

Countering Terrorism

"Zero-Tolerance Approach to Terrorism,"[8] has received singular emphasis under the current government of India and will be pursued diplomatically with the military being employed in case the former fails. First preference will be for international and regional engagement. Prime Minister Modi conveyed this approach at the Shanghai Cooperation Organisation (SCO) Summit held in June 2019 almost immediately after the swearing in of the government in the second term.[9] Pakistan is also a member of the SCO and thus the message was driven home in no uncertain terms. Towards this end, Pakistan given what Prime Minister Modi described as a deceitful state[10] will remain key focus of counter terror punitive response as a component of the defence policy for which an effective response will be built up. Terrorism and proxy war are also seen as tools that are employed by those not having the requisite conventional capability and has a global dimension. [11]

In terms of employment of armed forces this will envisage a punitive response that will be sustained in the years ahead. One of the first procurements made was emergency purchases for the Indian Air Force of Spice bunker bursting munitions which was successfully employed in the cross-border air strike at Balakot on 26 February 2019.[12] Coastal Security will also be weaved into the counter terrorism policy as this has been a major challenge and a gap that was exposed in the Mumbai 26/11 terrorist attack launched by Pakistan based Lashkar-e-Taiba terrorists, who approached the commercial capital from the sea. The steps underlined are for establishing a National Committee for Strengthening Maritime & Coastal Security, Island Information System and National Academy of Coastal Policing.

Defence Cooperation

Cooperation to counter terrorism with strategic partners will be a core theme in defence relations. Maritime cooperation is another dimension of the approach with a view to ensuring safety and security of sea lanes, preventing maritime piracy and crime and ensuring security of oil and gas tankers passing through the Persian Gulf. Indian Navy, however, is unlikely to join any grouping for this purpose but is likely to operate independently. Humanitarian Assistance and Disaster Relief is another dimension with demonstrated capabilities of the Indian Navy evident since the Great Tsunami of 2004 and displayed in Mozambique in March April 2019 to assist the nation in facing the vagaries arising from Cyclone Idai. Indian Navy had also launched 'Operation Vanilla' to assist the population of Madagascar affected by Cyclone Diane in 2020. The world of opportunities lies in expanding cooperation with India in the field of defence and security.

Jointness and Innovation in Defence Organisations and Operations

Indian armed forces face a major challenge from the siloed and single service approach be it for operations or logistics. The Prime Minister has emphasised on jointness amongst the three arms of the armed forces, an issue specifically emphasised by the Prime Minister during Kargil Vijay Diwas function in Delhi in July 2019. [13] This will remain a focus in the coming years. Towards imparting greater efficiency and ensuing effectiveness, restructuring exercises have been undertaken by the armed forces. The aim is to cut flab, for instance Indian Army plans to reduce numbers and provide a fillip to capital acquisitions which have been hampered due to skewed ratio of expenditure on personnel both serving and veterans that is taking a major chunk of the defence budget. The dilemma for the land forces will remain juggling the boots on the ground required for fighting the two Ms – militancy and mountains while acquiring the third M - modern weapon systems. As declared in the Indian Army Land Warfare Doctrine 2018, the Indian Army will continue to optimise its resources and forces, "based on the present and future challenges and will be structured to be an agile, mobile and technology driven force, operating in synergy with the other services".[14]

The Army is reviewing holding and reserves of ammunition, equipment and other stocks as per envisaged operational role and likely employment of each soldier/ sub-unit/ unit/ formation at various stages of battle tailored to specific threats says the doctrine.[15] The Indian Navy has adopted Mission Based Deployment in the Indian Ocean Region where extra territorial navies are fielding submarines and establishing bases. With emphasis on fielding a full complement of 135 ships for operations, the effective cycle in terms of training and maintenance is ensured so that requisite numbers are available to undertake missions as counter piracy, escorting of oil tankers and maritime crime and terrorism. Validation of the capabilities through real time exercises will also be emphasised. For instance, Indian Air Force conducted exercise *Gagan Shakti* successfully validating ability to manage operations simultaneously on two fronts in 2018. Yet the dwindling number of fighter squadrons meant that the IAF (Indian Air Force) will remain two thirds of the desired strength for some years to come and thus enhancing the pace of accretions will remain a key priority in defence capability building.

Defence Acquisitions, Production, Research & Development

Amidst the growing two-front challenge from Pakistan and China, the government will have to take considered decisions to ensure that the cutting edge of the armed forces is retained. Speeding up purchases to make up deficiencies in the defence equipment through self-reliance is core focus of the defence policy. The emphasis on Make in India in defence that was the buzzword introduced by Prime Minister Narendra Modi in 2014 is continuing till date . At the same time employment generation will remain a key factor through indigenisation. The focus will be on privatisation of the defence industry with greater incentives being provided for this purpose while corporatisation of the government and public sector enterprises will be emphasised. To promote corporatisation of the

Defence Public Sector Undertakings (DPSUs) such as Bharat Electronics Limited (BEL) and BEML Ltd, disinvestment has been undertaken with the government shareholding in these DPSUs at 66.72 percent and 54.03 percent respectively.

For privatisation the 'Strategic Partnership (SP)' Model which envisages establishment of long-term strategic partnerships with Indian entities through a transparent and competitive process, wherein they would tie up with global Original Equipment Manufacturers (OEMs) to seek technology transfers to set up domestic manufacturing infrastructure and supply chain is likely to be the way ahead. A number of modifications are introduced in the Defence Procurement Procedure (DPP) to fast track procurements. Herein lies a world of opportunities for foreign state and private partners for collaboration in defence Research and Development (R&D) and production in India.

Budget: A Key Challenge

India being a developing country with a large population living below the poverty line, there will be an eternal crunch of funding for defence that is the " the guns versus butter dilemma". The budget of the government under Prime Minister Narendra Modi saw significant increase in allocations for Defence. "Defence has an immediate requirement of modernisation and upgradation. This is a national priority. For this purpose, imports of defence equipment that are not being manufactured in India are being exempted from the basic customs duty," the Finance Minister, Nirmala Sitharaman who is also the past Defence Minister had said earlier. The capital allocation made in the Budget is expected to only take care of the committed liabilities and leave little for new acquisitions. Lower Gross Domestic Products (GDP) accretion and need to kick start a number of infrastructure and related programmes for long-term investment in the priority development sector has no doubt constrained the Finance Minister. The COVID-19 pandemic could further aggravate India's funding dilemma for its defence modernisation.

Meanwhile, to overcome the paucity of resources, a change in the terms of reference of the Fifteenth Finance Commission (FfFC), to recommend apportioning a share of the Centre's tax collections to defence procurement and only then share balance with the States is now proposed. The FfFC which will be allocating resources proportionately between the centre and the states is expected to deduct funds to be made available for defence for the pool and then distribute the rest to the States. By this step the government hopes to have adequate resources for defence capability accretion without dipping into resources for development.

Conclusion

In the recent years, the government of India has undertaken some path breaking decisions in terms of demonstration of hard power such as the surgical strikes or the Shakti Anti Satellite tests. India's defence policy while pursuing a combination of proactive and reactive aggression is likely to focus on medium to long term capability building to strengthen deterrence. Towards this end, innovative funding, prioritising, restructuring and self-reliance will be main way ahead. Enforcing jointness on the armed forces working in their silos, promoting synergy and cooperative public-private foreign and indigenous collaboration in Research and Development and manufacturing could also produce desirable results in enhancing deterrence. The last named – collaborative Research, Development and manufacturing is the world of opportunities that India presents for strategic partners, governments and defense industry alike.

Endnotes

1   Surgical Strike refers to cross border/Line of Control special raids launched by the Indian Army and the Indian Air Force in September 2016 and February 2019 respectively at terrorist camps and launch pads in Pakistan Occupied Kashmir and Pakistan respectively.

2   Press Trust of India. (2018). India has never been an aggressor nor an encroacher: PM Modi. https://timesofindia.indiatimes.com/india/india-has-never-been-an-aggressor-nor-an-encroacher-pm-narendra-modi/articleshow/63976744.cms . Accessed 13 August, 2021.

3   Indian Army Land Warfare Doctrine. (2018). http://www.ssri-j.com/MediaReport/Document/IndianArmyLandWarfareDoctrine2018.pdf. Accessed 18 August, 2021.

4   Ministry of Defence Annual Report, Government of India. (2018). https://mod.gov.in/sites/default/files/MoDAR2018.pdf. Accessed 31 August, 2021.

5   Press Information Bureau. (2018). Peace is the pre-requisite for progress – Vice President of India. http://pib.nic.in/Pressreleaseshare.aspx?PRID=1549692/. Accessed 21 September, 2021.

6   Press Information Bureau. (2019). PM addresses Kargil Vijay Diwas commemorative function in New Delhi. https://pib.gov.in/Pressreleaseshare.aspx?PRID=1580568. Accessed 22 September, 2021.

7   Observations of the author made during various seminars in the national capital over the years.

8   Economic Times. (2019). Air Force Looks at Buying Advanced Bunker Buster Version of Spice 2000 Bombs. https://economictimes.indiatimes.com/news/defence/air-force-looks-at-buying-advanced-bunker-buster-version-of-spice-2000-bombs/articleshow/69229514.cms?from=mdr. Accessed 29 September, 2021.

9   Jayadeva Ranade. (2019). Modi Government Unveils India's Security Strategy. https://sniwire.com/defence-security/modi-government-unveils-indias-security-strategy/. Accessed 6 August, 2021.

10 Press Information Bureau. (2019). Op. cit.

11 Ibid.

12 Economic Times. (2019). Op. Cit.

13 Press Information Bureau. (2019).

14 Indian Army Land Warfare Doctrine. Op. Cit.

15 Ibid.

Chapter 5

Science and Technology Policy of India

Ajey Lele

Introduction

One of the foundational pillars in a country's development is its focus on Science and Technology (S&T). Although most countries join hands in collaboration influenced by political, economic, and cultural factors, the relationships formed by S&T continues further actively. To enhance S&T each country calls for cooperation with other countries both in terms of exchange of expertise and designing better solutions, developing relationships, and connecting countries. The Indian scientific community is bubbling with potential with their participation and excellence in areas such as space, biotechnology, green technology, and even disruptive technologies such as artificial intelligence and robotics. Amidst technology-driven countries like Japan, China, and the US, India holds a special place in the global arena. The Indian account of S&T can be classified into three aspects such as multilateral engagement with other countries, the economic standpoint of Indian services and the way India cooperates with other countries in the field of S&T. Following sections debate some important sectors, broadly traces the nature of investments made by India in those sectors, identifies the nature of international engagement for last few decades and looks at the ongoing efforts.

Space Science and Technology

India is one of the few developing countries in the field of developing space technology. Multiple other space organisations such as National

Aeronautics and Space Administration (NASA) of USA, European Space Agency (ESA) and Japan Aerospace Exploration Agency (JAXA) and many other space forums have collaborated with the Indian Space Research Organisation (ISRO) since its inception on 15 August 1969.

The principal segment of space cooperation between ISRO and the international community are in the fields of:

➤ Launch vehicle and launch services.

➤ Payloads and sensors - scientific and civilian mission.

➤ Space communications and infrastructure.

➤ Tracking and data reception facilities.[1]

From the beginning of its space program, India played an active role in pushing to keep Outer Space beyond interstate conflicts. This change in focus of India's space program has steered India to pursue collaborative ventures in space with space powers such as the US, Japan, and France. India and Europe are massively investing in outer space, and both have significant economic stakes in keeping the Outer Space environment clear, guarded, and maintained. India's investments are worth USD 37 billion, including the ground-based infrastructure and value-added services.[2] Therefore, the security of its space assets is of high priority. The EU-India cooperation agreement in March 2018 presents an invaluable opportunity to produce mutual benefits, especially in the pursuit of:

1. The United Nations' Sustainable Development Goals

2. To share Earth Observation Satellite Data

3. long–term collaboration on data processing for shared use in line with the EU-India Agenda for Action 2020

4. Agreed intention for the active development of downstream sectors in EU and India.[3]

Europe and India possess their capacities in the areas of earth observation and communication satellites. Another significant area for India and Europe to come together would be for extending space development assistance to a number of emerging space players in Asia, Africa, and Latin America. The Indian space agency, Indian Space Research Organisation (ISRO) and the French National Space Agency (CNES) have been undertaking joint missions such as Megha-Tropiques and Saral-Altika. The two also have ongoing initiatives such as the Trishna satellite for land Infrared monitoring and the Oceansat-3 Argos mission.[4] Arianespace (France) was the leading partner for ISRO's Heavy Satellite launches. India and the USA have collaborated through their space wings ISRO and NASA, respectively, in the NASA-ISRO Synthetic Aperture Radar (NISAR) mission to develop and launch a dual-frequency (L, S bands) Polarimetric Synthetic Aperture Radar. This would help in remote sensing and assist in recognising and learning natural processes on Earth.[5] This mission is planned to be launched by 2024. Through the Mangalyaan mission in 2013, India and the USA joined in telemetry and tracking for deep space network during MOM launch monitoring (Ibid).[6] Marking the 40th anniversary of the Aryabhata launch by a Soyuz launch vehicle by the then USSR, Russia's ROSCOSMOS and ISRO have signed an MoU on expanding their cooperation in the field of exploration and the peaceful use of outer space in June 2015.[7] Outer Space collaboration has been at the forefront in the India-Canada bilateral relations. India and Canada have been collaborating in the areas of space, earth observation, satellite launch services, and ground support for space missions.

Space market has typically been somewhat restrictive for private actors' involvement in India. The government of India has adopted business-friendly policies under its recent flagship initiatives that can ease the doing-of-business for foreign space industries, such as raising the cap on foreign direct investment (FDI) in the space sector from 49% to 100%, as part of a broader initiative (Make in India) that seeks to position India as a global manufacturing hub.[8] The Union Budget of 2019 focused on harnessing the emerging business opportunity for India in launching satellites and other space products. Eyeing the commercial benefits, the Indian government has established Public Sector Enterprise (PSE) as New Space India Limited (NSIL), which functions as a supplementary commercial arm under the Department of Space. NSIL taps into the gains by the R&D carried out by ISRO, thereby marketing the space products in the global market including the production of launch vehicles, the transfer of technologies and the marketing of these new products.[9] While India is one of the Big Six in Space, it has yet to unroll a national policy for the robust participation of the private industry in the space sector. This can be complemented with a space command with a legal architecture such as Space Act with ISRO in the forefront.[10] India's market has vast untapped potential when it comes to space products and services, and it is waiting to be unveiled.

Cyberspace

The Indian cyberspace or the internet ecosystem has vastly developed in the last two decades. India was among the top five countries to be affected by cybercrimes as a report by the Symantec Corp suggested.[11] Amidst cyber espionage and exploitation through phishing is on the rise, India has tremendous potential to grow. India also ranks 3rd globally with the highest number of internet users in the world after the USA and China,[12] simultaneously with numerous cyberattacks in the recent past have opened up vulnerabilities in the Indian cybersecurity platform. In May 2019, the introduction of the Defence Cyber Agency was announced, by Prime Minister Narendra Modi. It is part of the three new tri-service agencies, for cyber warfare, space, and special operations.[13] It is set up to work in conjunction with the National Cyber Security Advisor, focusing solely on military issues. Being introduced under the National Cyber Security Policy (2013), it is to ensure the security and resilience in the cyberspace for civilians, businesses, and the government. Being a tri-service agency, it will consist of personnel from all the three arms of the Indian defence forces, army, navy, and air force.[14]

India and Canada have advanced their cooperation in the cyberspace in recent years. A Memorandum of Understanding signed between the Ministry of Communication and IT of India and the Department of Public Safety and Emergency Preparedness of Canada on the cooperation in the area of cybersecurity in March 2015.[15] In addition, Canada and India also have in place a mutual legal assistance treaty (MLAT). The MLAT is in force since 1995. Other countries who have matched to a shared vision include Qatar and the United Arab Emirates. In 2017, the two Gulf countries joined hands with India for a protocol on technical cooperation in the field of cybersecurity to fight cybercrimes.[16] Also, during the third India-Japan Cyber Dialogue in February 2019, discussions were held on issues relating to cybersecurity enhancements, in order to create an open, free, secure, and stable cyberspace.[17] As per a study by Capgemini Digital Transformation Institute (2018), India and the United States have the largest cyber security talent pool out of nine countries surveyed including the United Kingdom, France, Italy, Spain, the Netherlands, and Germany.

The aforementioned proves India's competence with skilled labour.[18] The World Economic Forum (WEF) ranking in its Global Risk Report revealed India had suffered the largest data breach in the world due to 'lax cyber security protocols'.[19] This can undoubtedly be explained as India still lacks a comprehensive cyber security policy to protect the critical infrastructure of many sectors.

Artificial Intelligence

Among disruptive technologies, "Artificial Intelligence" (AI) takes a centre-stage and a significant advancement for the future. India having understood the impact of AI towards easing the operational difficulties in sectors such as banking and finance, energy, healthcare, manufacturing, logistics and transport, education, and tourism is found giving greater emphasis towards development of this technology. India's efforts to incorporate AI in various sectors got highlighted with NITI Aayog announcing the proposal for a national policy on artificial intelligence, to counter China's momentum towards AI.[20] It is expected to draft a short-term, medium-term and long-term goal plan. Specific areas where AI could be implemented have been identified, such as agriculture, health, education, banking, and transportation. The funding for the program would be allocated under the Atal Innovation Mission.[21].

Although India does not have much achievement under its belt with respect to AI, however, the National Union Budget focusses on AI development, along with many others. The Government of India plans to train 10 million in industry-relevant skills such as AI, Internet-of-Things and Big Data.[22] India, on the other hand, has cooperated in the field of AI, between India's Department of Science (DST) and Japan's Science and Technology Agency (JST). Under the DST-JST cooperation framework, three new India-Japan Joint Laboratories were approved and initiated in the areas of AI, data analytics, and cybersecurity.[23] India and China, through the Sino-Indian Digital Collaboration Plaza (SIDCOP), had decided to join hands to launch their first joint projects in the field of AI and Big Data. The projects, initiated by China and India's National Association for Software and Services Companies (NASSCOM), intend to promote collaboration between Indian software companies and Chinese firms in high-tech manufacturing in Big Data and IoT projects.[24] While China leads Asia in AI investments, the markets of both countries are varied and unequal.

Robotics

The Department of Telecommunication (DoT) in 2018 had released a draft telecom policy aiming to create a roadmap for emerging technologies such as 5G, robotics, AI, IoT, and cloud computing.[25] While other countries have devised a comprehensive national policy for robotics, India seems to be in the beginning stages in adopting and advancing in robotics. With countries like Japan and China having their own robotics programs pushing forward in the 21st century, South Korea has collaborations with India in the robotics arena. With the establishment of the Robot Revolution Initiative Council by Prime Minister Shinzo Abe, Japan plans to utilise robotics in every corner of the Japanese economy and society.[26]

The reasoning for advancement in robotics in China and Japan is due to the fall of the working-age population. While in China it dropped by 3.7 million in 2014, in the case of Japan, a quarter of the population is above the age of 65.[27] But India does not have such a demographic problem such as the others. Over the years, the Indian robotics enterprise has advanced beyond traditional business areas, such as manufacturing and production, to enter emerging domains including education, rehabilitation, and entertainment. Across the same time span, the robotics researchers and educators in India have grown from just a few to several hundred skilled professionals working in the industry, higher education, and energy organisations. Currently, robotics in India is developed through entrepreneurship and start-ups, usually self-funded, or through private equity, or venture capital.[28] India possesses many of the basic elements in place to become a robotics industry force, including a sound educational system, established business and academic research facilities, and an increasingly entrepreneurial business community. The reason for India to focus on robotics stems from the fact that India faces an unprecedented rate of *brain drain*.

Green Technology

Green Technology has been a focus area in technological innovations in recent years. Climate change-led environmental degradation has become a significant threat to flora and fauna. The narrative of growth and climate goals are opposed to each other and have started to wane away with the introduction of green economy and thereby green technologies. The so-called green race has already begun wherein countries have positioned themselves to focus on growth while taking care of their environment.[29]

India has a long way to go in the global green race. While other countries have a significant head-start in the green sector, India with its innovative and technical mindset, would be able to adapt swifter than the rest. India has a notable industry with low-carbon environmental goods and services (LCEGS).[30] Being the third-largest energy consumer in the world, the International Energy Agency (IEA) proposes that India has the capacity to add almost 30 percent to the global energy demand growth by 2040. It includes an increase in global energy consumption from 6 percent in 2018, to 11 percent by 2040.[31] This has led to the formulation of a roadmap for the future of India by Oil and Natural Gas Corporation called Strategic Roadmap 2040.[32]

The Union Budget proposed the support for entrepreneurs in encouraging farmers to produce energy from solar installations.[33] While the Economic Survey inferred that India would require USD 250 billion between 2023 and 2030 to assure progression within a green economy.[34] This comes at a time when the Organization of the Petroleum Exporting Countries (OPEC) has hinted at production cuts.[35] India plans to reduce its carbon footprint by 33-35 percent from its 2005 levels by 2030.[36] India's necessity to become energy efficient stems from the fact that it is one of the biggest emitters of greenhouse gases after China and the US, making them extremely vulnerable to climate change and their implications. India also has its commitments to the United Nations Framework Convention on Climate Change adopted by 195 countries in Paris in 2015. While India is ranked fourth in wind energy capacity and fifth in solar power capacity, there is a lot more ground to cover in terms of policy formulation for India's position in the global green race.

Biotechnology

Karl Ereky, a Hungarian engineer, first coined the term biotechnology in 1919. India's Biotechnology Industry is currently among the top twelve destinations in the world and ranks third in the Asia-Pacific region. It also holds 2 percent of the global market share. This industry is divided into five segments, which are bio-pharmaceuticals, bio-services, bio-agriculture, bio-industrials, and bio-IT.[37] India through the years has grown extensively in this field and has set up the National Biotechnology Development Strategy (NBDS 2015-20). They also want to ensure coherence between various skills across sectors, with a major focus on research in basic, disciplinary, and inter-disciplinary science.[38] Under Mission Innovation the first Clean Energy International Incubator program has been set up which provides start-ups from 23 participating EU countries to develop and incubate in India and furthermore, start-ups from such incubators can partner with other countries enabling access to global prospects.[39] A Letter of Intent was signed on 15 April 2015 between the Department of Biotechnology (DBT), Ministry of Science and Technology and Grand Challenges of Canada (GCC) regarding the implementation of DBT-GCC collaboration in Disease Elimination and Saving Brains initiative.[40]

Under the FDI policy of India, 100 percent FDI is allowed under the automatic route in pharmaceuticals for Greenfield projects, as well as medical devices. Numerous investment opportunities have opened up in India in drug discovery and clinical trials, medical devices manufacturing, biosimilars, and secondary agriculture with investors in this field ranging from Bosch (Germany), Tekes (Finland), Mylan (USA), GE Healthcare (USA), Limagrain (France), and Abbott Laboratories (USA).[41] India has showcased its potential in the field of biotechnology and new business opportunities to collaborate. It shows the importance placed on the advancement in the field to sustain a future where India turns into a leading country in the field. India requires a stronger institutional capacity with a redesigned governance model, particularly for biotechnology.

The Road Ahead

India has the unique opportunity to become global leader in every field of S&T. India has a population demographics which will surpass China in the near future, with more than half the population under age 30 and less than one-fourth aging 45 or older. The implications can definitely lead to the meteoric rise of a country like India maintaining friendly ties and building partnerships with every other country. Significant decisions that the Indian government undertakes under the leadership of Prime Minister Narendra Modi will pave the path for the future and build a foundation for the strategic S&T preparation in the following decades. Considering the numerous ways, India has collaborated with other countries in areas of S&T, space, cybersecurity, biotechnology, among others, there is still a lot left to aspire. Furthermore, this could open up vast opportunities for India in areas of interest such as agriculture, ICT, space, cleantech, and many more. Eyeing the importance of the Indo-Pacific region in the future of global power dynamics, India, a rising influence, recognises the opportunity of collaborating in areas of interests with other countries. It is particularly accurate in the current climate of a tech trade war between the USA and China, and India can carve its own space for its technology requirements. What India demands more than ever, and the strategies the incumbent Modi government should focus on would be to find a stable and competent partner in the fields of ICT and outer space. It is essential not to get pulled into the scuffle between the US and China, but rather keep India's interests in mind and focus on leveraging better opportunities afforded by the tech-hungry country like India. From the ever-growing cyberspace in India, to the ISRO being a provider of cost-effective satellite launch systems to other countries, India has demonstrated a promising business opportunity from a global perspective. In space sector India has global acceptability owing the various successes achieved by India's space agency. India is proposing a model of public-private partnership to manage maximum gain from this sector. Indian private players in the space industry have major challenges as well as opportunities ahead. The introduction of NSIL in the Union Budget of 2019 could lead the private players to perform a more prominent part in space products in unison with the Department of Space which as proposed will focus on R&D by ISRO.[42] By devising a comprehensive Space Policy to go along with the commercial aspect, India could benefit from the business and scientific profits it could deliver.

Apart from the existing fields of collaboration, India can assist in the areas of cost-effective R&D in healthcare and industrial infrastructure for other countries, along with comprehensive cybersecurity cooperation. Being the leading force in the IT sector with major software exports around the world, India can continue to play a major role in IT sector also and expand the footprint with adequate assistance from Modi government. With the largest trained manpower in software, India with its companies has invested in foundational technologies such as Operating Systems (OS), chip design, firewalls, routers, etc. The government can bring up a major change industry environment and attract investments by using policies and structures made available for initiatives like "Start-Up" India and "Make-In-India" initiatives. There is a major need for the government to ensure significant growth in foreign investments in various technological sectors. Also, there is a need to engage Indian diaspora very effectively at various levels. They can contribute both in terms of investments and expertise. Also, healthy transfer of knowledge in various newer arenas of technologies like internet of things (LoT), Blockchain and 3D printing should be ensured. Prime Minister Modi has announced the goal of making India a US$5 trillion economy by 2024. This is possible when the industrialisation process gets going with sound S & T support.

Endnotes

1   Mukherjee, Amit. (2018). ISPRS Annals of the Photogrammetry, Remote Sensing and Spatial Information Sciences, Volume IV-5., International Cooperation In Space Technology: An Abstraction With Fuzzy Logic Analysis. https://www.isprs-ann-photogramm-remote-sens-spatial-inf-sci. net/IV-5/13/2018/isprs-annals-IV-5-13-2018.pdf, accessed on 30 June 2019.

2   Pillai, Rajeshwari. (2019). ESPI Report on Europe India Space Cooperation: Policy, Legal and Business Perspectives from India. India-Europe Space Security Cooperation, https://espi.or.at/publications/espi-public-reports/ send/2-public-espi-reports/453-europe-india-space-cooperation-policy-legal-and-business-perspectives-from-india, accessed on 26 June 2019.

3   Ibid.

4   Ibid.

5   Mukherjee, Amit. (2018). Op. Cit.

6   Ibid.

7   Press Information Bureau, Government of India (2015). Space co-operation agreement between India and Russia. http://pib.nic.in/newsite/PrintRelease. aspx?relid=123593, accessed on 3 July 2019.

8   Prasad, Narayan. (2019). ESPI Report on Europe India Space Cooperation: Policy, Legal and Business Perspectives from India. New Space in India: Assessing its potential and engagement opportunities with Europe. https:// espi.or.at/publications/espi-public-reports/send/2-public-espi-reports/453-europe-india-space-cooperation-policy-legal-and-business-perspectives-from-india, accessed on 26 June 2019.

9   Ministry of Finance, Union Budget Speech. (2019) https://www.indiabudget. gov.in/budgetspeech.php, accessed on 6 July 2019.

10 Lele, Ajey. (2016). India's Space Security Policy: A Proposal. IDSA. https:// idsa.in/policybrief/indias-space-security-policy_alele_280416, accessed on 2 July 2019.

11 Symantec Corp. (2019) Internet Security Threat Report Volume 24.https:// www.symantec.com/content/dam/symantec/docs/reports/istr-24-2019-en. pdf, accessed on 3 July 2019.

12 NITI Aayog (2019). Cyber Security. , https://niti.gov.in/writereaddata/files/ document_publication/CyberSecurityConclaveAtVigyanBhavanDelhi_1. pdf, accessed on 3 July 2019.

13 Mitra, Prarthana. (2019). QRIUS, India is setting up Defence Cyber Agency. What will it do? https://qrius.com/india-is-setting-up-defence-cyber-agency-what-will-it-do/, accessed on 29 June 2019.

14 Asian News International (2019). India to have Defence Cyber Agency in May; Rear Admiral Mohit to be its first chief, https://www.indiatoday.in/india/story/india-defence-cyber-agency-may-rear-admiral-mohit-1513381-2019-04-30, accessed on 2 July 2019.

15 Gateway House (2019). Opportunities for Cooperative Cyber Security. https://www.gatewayhouse.in/wp-content/uploads/2019/02/Canada-India-Paper-No.1_0.pdf, accessed on 30 June 2019.

16 Ministry of External Affairs, Annual Report 2016-17. http://www.mea.gov.in/Uploads/PublicationDocs/29521_MEA_ANNUAL_REPORT_2016_17_new.pdf, accessed on 29 June 2019.

17 Ministry of External Affairs. (2019) Third India-Japan Cyber Dialogue. https://www.mea.gov.in/press-releases.htm?dtl/31107/Third+IndiaJapan+Cyber+Dialogue, accessed on 2 July 2019.

18 Capgemini Digital Transformation Institute. (2018). Cybersecurity Talent-The Big Gap in Cyber Protection. https://www.capgemini.com/wp-content/uploads/2018/02/the-cybersecurity-talent-gap-v8_web.pdf, accessed on 30 June 2019.

19 World Economic Forum. (2019). Global Risk Report.http://www3.weforum.org/docs/WEF_Global_Risks_Report_2019.pdf, accessed on 2 July 2019.

20 NITI Aayog. (2018) National Strategy for Artificial Intelligence. https://niti.gov.in/writereaddata/files/document_publication/NationalStrategy-for-AI-Discussion-Paper.pdf, accessed on 29 June 2019.

21 Ibid.

22 Ministry of Finance, Union Budget Speech 2019. https://www.indiabudget.gov.in/budgetspeech.php, accessed on 6 July 2019.

23 Department of Science and Technology, Annual Report 2017-18. https://drive.google.com/file/d/1IPKUdbSx0Da2Zi_ufzC4u-T3jCFzPred/view?usp=sharing, accessed on 28 June 2019.

24 Press Information Bureau. (2019). Launch of Sino-Indian Digital Collaboration Plaza. http://pib.nic.in/PressReleaseIframePage.aspx?PRID=1559382, accessed on 3 July 2019.

25 Department of Telecommunications, National Digital Communications Policy-2018. http://dot.gov.in/sites/default/files/Final%20NDCP-2018.pdf?download=1, accessed on 2 July 2019.

26   Prakash Aseem. (2016). Robotics Business Review, In Asian Robotics Industry Race, India Goes Its Own Way. https://www.roboticsbusinessreview.com/manufacturing/in_asian_robotics_industry_race_india_goes_its_own_way/, accessed on 3 July 2019.

27   Ibid.

28   Edwards, John. (2016). Robotics Business Review, Robotics in India Starts Small but is Growing Fast.https://www.roboticsbusinessreview.com/supply-chain/robotics_in_india_starts_small_but_is_growing_fast/, accessed on 3 July 2019.

29   Kirton, David. (2019). Caixin, China's Solar-Panel Makers Dominate Global Exports.   https://www.caixinglobal.com/2019-01-24/chinas-solar-panel-makers-dominate-global-exports-101374069.html,   accessed   on   27   June 2019.

30   Srivatav, Sugandha & Kathuria, Rajat. (2018). Green technology: Can India win the race?https://www.financialexpress.com/opinion/green-technology-can-india-win-the-race/1126192/, accessed on 2 July 2019.

31   International Energy Agency, World Energy Outlook 2017. Global Shifts in Energy System, https://www.iea.org/weo2017/, accessed on 2 July 2019.

32   The Telegraph (2019).   ONGC to re-draw vision document. https://www.telegraphindia.com/business/ongc-to-re-draw-vision-document/cid/1682859, accessed on 9 July 2019.

33   Ministry of Finance, Union Budget Speech 2019. https://www.indiabudget.gov.in/budgetspeech.php, accessed on 6 July 2019.

34   Ministry of Finance, Economic Survey 2018-19.Volume 1.https://www.indiabudget.gov.in/economicsurvey/doc/vol1chapter/echap09_vol1.pdf, accessed on 12 July 2019.

35   Faucon, Benoit & Said, Summer. (2019). The Wall Street Journal, Despite Mideast Tensions, OPEC Inches Closer to Maintaining Production Cuts Through 2019. https://www.wsj.com/articles/despite-mideast-tensions-opec-inches-closer-to-maintaining-production-cuts-through-2019-11558282225, accessed on 2 July 2019.

36   Ministry of Environment, Forest and Climate Change (2015). India's Intended Nationally Determined Contribution: Working Towards Climate Justice.http://nmhs.org.in/pdf/INDIA%20INDC%20TO%20UNFCCC.pdf, accessed on 3 July 2019.

37 Make In India Website, India's Biotechnology Sector.http://www.
makeinindia.com/sector/biotechnology, accessed on 9 July 2019.

38 Ibid.

39 Department of Science and Technology, Annual Report 2017-18. https://
drive.google.com/file/d/1IPKUdbSx0Da2Zi_ufzC4u-T3jCFzPred/
view?usp=sharing, accessed on 30 June 2019.

40 Ministry of External Affairs, Annual Report 2015-16. https://www.mea.
gov.in/Uploads/PublicationDocs/26525_26525_External_Affairs_English_
AR_2015-16_Final_compressed.pdf, accessed on 30 June 2019.

41 Make in India Website, India's Biotechnology Sector. http://www.
makeinindia.com/sector/biotechnology, accessed on 10 July 2019.

42 Ministry of Finance, Union Budget Speech 2019. https://www.indiabudget.
gov.in/budgetspeech.php, accessed on 16 July 2019.

Chapter 6

Defence Reforms under the Narendra Modi Government

Ghanshyam Singh Katoch

"If you call yourself a leader, then you have to be decisive. If you're decisive, then you have the chance to be a leader. These are two sides to the same coin".

> *- Narendra Modi (Interview with Reuters in 2013 when Chief Minister of Gujarat State)*

Introduction

Narendra Damodardas Modi became the Prime Minister (PM) of India in May 2014 with a reputation of a no-nonsense, decisive strongman, as also the choice for PM of a party which prides itself on a right-wing nationalist discourse, a flavour of the world at the present times. The Defence Services were optimistic that years of being resource constrained were going to end. It was only in Dec 2014 that a clearer view of his thinking on the Defence Services as the strong arm of national security emerged. On 17 October 2014, the PM addressed his first Combined Commanders Conference at New Delhi which is held annually and attended by the topmost commanders of the army, navy and air force. What the PM states at the conference is obviously vetted by him after it is prepared for him by his staff which includes the PM's Office, the National Security Advisor (NSA), the Ministry of Defence (MoD), the Head Quarter Integrated Defence Staff (HQ IDS) and the National Security Council Secretariat. While the speech necessarily is shrouded in the ambiguity required in public speeches involving the nation's core security interests and policy, nevertheless, reading between the lines, the security philosophy and the direction in which security related policies will move, can be broadly perceived. During the 2014 conference, two statements by PM Modi which merited attention were, "full-scale wars may become rare, but force will remain an instrument of deterrence and influencing behaviour, and the duration of conflicts will be shorter", and "focus on efficiency and economy in the use of resources and our military assets, including greater integration and sharing of resources among the Services and draw up long term acquisition plans keeping in view availability of resources, future operational requirements and technology trends".[1] The portents from these words for the future defence policy of India were, firstly, meant that India would use the military as an instrument of deterrence without prolonging any military action. Secondly, the defence budget would not be enhanced and instead measures would be taken to synergise existing assets with greater synergy and technology.

India's Defence Policy under the Narendra Modi Government

During December 2015, while addressing the Combined Commanders Conference 2015 onboard the aircraft carrier INS Vikramaditya (in line with his directions of 2014 that the Combined Commanders Conference should preferably be held outside New Delhi), Prime Minister Narendra Modi, who by then had a greater insight into military-related security affairs made the following important points:[2]

➢ He stated that "India's history has been influenced by the seas. And, the passage to our future prosperity and security also lies on this [Indian] ocean."

➢ He paid tribute to the Central Armed Police Forces (CAPFs) whose task is internal security including counter-terrorism and counter-insurgency as he stated "their valour and sacrifices defeat terrorism in Jammu and Kashmir, reduce the violence of Left-Wing Extremism and keep our Northeast more peaceful."

➢ He stated that "[in] an inter-dependent world, India's transformation is closely linked with our international partnerships."

➢ Speaking of Russia and the USA he said, "Russia has always been a source of strength for us. With the United States, we have advanced our partnership in a comprehensive manner, including in defence. Our strategic partnerships in Europe have deepened."

➢ He referred to the importance of India's neighbourhood which he said, "is most critical for our future and for our place in the world." He also said that this includes China with whom "we will aim to address outstanding issues, maintain stability on the border and develop greater mutual understanding and trust in our overlapping neighbourhood."

➢ He stressed upon building domestic capabilities without which no country can be a great power. Such an endeavour "will also reduce capital costs and inventories. In addition, it will be a huge catalyst for industry, employment and economic growth in India".

➢ He directly addressed the increasing size of the Defence forces as a problem and said that 'modernisation and expansion of forces at the same time is a difficult and unnecessary goal. We need forces that are agile, mobile and driven by technology, not just human valour."

➢ He said that we need capabilities to win swift wars, "for we will not have the luxury of long drawn battles", and "as our security horizons and responsibilities extend beyond our shores and borders, we must prepare our forces for range and mobility."

➢ Lastly, he again emphasised on a point which he had made in the 2014 conference about lack of jointness in the Defence forces by stating that "we wear different colours, but we serve the same cause and bear the same flag. Jointness at the top is a need that is long overdue."

Clearly, the PM had firmed his views on the way national security should be handled, views which were complemented by his handpicked National Security Advisor (NSA), Ajit Doval. Reading between the lines his words alluded to the following trajectory of Defence Reforms:

➢ A stress towards the sea and maritime power projection and diplomacy, and the ability of operating away from Indian shores.

➢ His importance to the Central Armed Police Forces (CAPF) in fighting proxy wars and protecting the country's internal cohesion.

In his line of thinking there is much in common between the military and the CAPFs and they need to work in unison. As do the three military Services.

➢ In security affairs, India would walk the fine line between Russia and the US and use both in resolving security issues especially with China. India would favour multilateral groupings to balance its security needs vis-a-vis China.

➢ He made it clear that the defence forces, the army needed downsizing through adoption of technology to enhance reach and efficiency.

➢ The finality of weaning away from foreign defence purchases by developing indigenous capabilities.

In fact, before December 2015 conference the Ministry of Defence (MoD) in the first year of PM Modi's tenure ordered a study to enhance combat capability and rebalance defence expenditure of the armed forces. It was headed by Lt Gen VG Sheketkar (Retd). The committee known in the media as the Sheketkar Committee gave several recommendations to streamline the military including its recommendation to reduce the numbers in the support services of the army. Concurrently, Mr Modi and his NSA were also looking at the Higher Defence Organisation in India which probably appeared sluggish to them. In April 2018 finally, India's defence planning architecture underwent a significant change with the Narendra Modi government deciding to establish an overarching defence planning committee (DPC) under the NSA. The aim was to leverage this cross-governmental body comprising the Chairman of the chiefs of staff committee, three service chiefs, the defence, expenditure and foreign secretaries, to enhance India's ability to facilitate comprehensive and integrated defence planning, which has been a grey area in the MoD's planning mechanism.[3] The NSA also replaced the cabinet secretary as the chairman of the strategic policy group (SPG), one of the three-tier structures of the Prime Minister-led National Security Council (NSC). This gives the NSA vast powers to exercise which he has been elevated to the rank of a cabinet minister. The NSA also got three deputy NSA's and a military advisor where there had earlier been only one NSA, and the post of the military advisor was vacant for a couple of years. What was noteworthy was that one Deputy NSA has been specifically tasked for technology based intelligence.

The Prime Minister's focus on efficiency and economy in the use of resources mentioned earlier also drew his attention to bringing in digital efficiency in the armed forces. He asked the services to give serious thought to upgrade technological skills for effective projection of power.[4] But besides the stress towards modernisation, which in due course got slowed down due to bureaucratic and economic reasons, the most important contribution of Modi government's first term was bringing in proactive responses to terrorist attacks on India. On 4 June 2015 post an ambush on an Indian army convoy in Manipur state in which 18 soldiers were killed, the PM authorised an attack across the Myanmar border to target the insurgents responsible. Back channel diplomacy was obviously used to assuage the Myanmar government as such operations across borders unless previously agreed upon are taken as an affront to a country's sovereignty. The attacks were given wide publicity in India which prompted statements from Pakistan which was apprehensive but confident that India wouldn't do a similar thing in response to an attack by its proxy terrorists. Pakistan's interior minister Chaudhry Nisar Ali Khan and top military commanders responded to remarks by an Indian minister that the raid by Special Forces against militants inside Myanmar was a message to Pakistan and groups "harbouring terror intent towards India". Khan said India should not mistake Pakistan for Myanmar. He warned that the "The Pakistan Army is fully capable of responding to any adventurism."[5]

On 18 September 2016, terrorists from the Pakistan based terrorist organisation Jaish-e-Muhammad attacked an Indian army camp at Uri (J&K) near the Line of Control (LoC). In the attack 19 Indian soldiers were killed. On 29 September, the Indian army informed the press that on night 28-29 September 2016, the outrage at Uri had been avenged by a "surgical strike' on terrorist camps across the LoC in which a large number of them were killed in a 40 minute operation in which special forces stuck at least 2 km inside Pakistan Occupied Jammu and Kashmir (POJK). The deterrence game between India and Pakistan had changed by India taking the upper hand in escalation dominance. So far, it was Pakistan that controlled escalation as was evidenced time and again through its sponsorship and direction of terrorist strikes in India.

The power that controls dominance also takes the risk of enlarging the war. India took the risk and validated that such strikes could be carried out by calling the Pakistani nuclear bluff. The term "surgical strike' has become very popular, having been used in many contexts since then mainly to denote a powerful response and an element of surprise from India. As a defence analyst stated, "the general consensus on deterrence and escalation in the region so far was that it was focused much more on the constraints facing India than that facing Pakistan. This was the consequence of Pakistan's effective use of the threat of nuclear escalation and the concern, particularly among Indian decision makers, that Pakistan was an irrational actor whose nuclear threats needed to be taken seriously."[6]

Near the end of his first term, PM Modi once again showed his grasp of escalation dominance by ordering an air strike on terrorist training camps in Pakistan, as opposed to the belief on both sides of the border that surgical strikes would be restricted to POJK. The air strike on a terrorist camp at Balakot, Pakistan came in the early hours of 26 February 2019, as retaliation to a particularly devastating car bomb attack on a CAPF convoy in the Kashmir Valley on 14 February 2019. The attack which killed 46 policemen re-joining their units after leave was the trigger for this "surgical strike". While in September 2016 the Pakistanis had denied any strikes inside POJK by India, in this case denial was not possible as the truth could not be hidden from Pakistan's own citizens. Stung by an affront to its sovereignty Pakistan stuck the next day "near Indian LoC military camps," from its own side of the LoC. It obviously didn't want to enlarge the conflict as it deliberately stuck 'near' the camps and not on the camps. India lost a vintage upgraded MIG-21 jet fighter in air-to-air combat as one MIG in the heat of the dogfight crossed across the LoC. Reportedly, a Pakistani F-16 was shot down, which was denied by Pakistan.

Modi's Second Term

PM Narendra Modi became PM for a second term, being sworn in on 31 May 2019, consequent to a landslide victory, after a bitterly fought election where national security was the core issue. The escalation dominance of Modi's first tenure points towards Narendra Modi seeking to keep this ace up his sleeve with greater confidence in the second term. The distinctive approach to Defence and security issues demonstrated by Modi's earlier administration will be further built up and refined. Journalist and defence analyst Nitin Gokhale quotes a former diplomat Amit Dasgupta in his book "Securing India the Modi Way" that "to achieve his strategic vision, Modi opted for his own distinctive approach: and second he opted to be disruptive and unpredictable and if required, unhesitatingly forceful. Both depart dramatically from the approach adopted by his predecessors. Such behaviour has planted in the Pakistani mind an aura of irrationality in Narendra Modi's response. Because of this they can no longer be sure of India's traditional restraint.[7]

In the Hindu epic, The Mahabharata, there is a story about a cousin of Lord Krishna, Shishupal, who was destined to die at the hands of Lord Krishna. Shishupala's mother took a boon from Lord Krishna that the Lord would pardon a hundred sins of Shishupala. Shishupala had fallen out with Lord Krishna and repeatedly committed offences against him. Lord Krishna kept on tolerating his offences till the 100th offence. When he committed the 101st offence, he was killed by Lord Krishna. From this story flows the Shisupala doctrine. This doctrine posits tolerating pin pricks till a limit is reached. Thereafter, a pin prick is replied with a sledgehammer blow. Some have likened PM Modi's style of functioning in line with this doctrine, and are confident that where "the combination of a strategy of rising retribution and seeking rapprochement, while at the same time pushing wide the asymmetry gap, when applied with two favourable governments, there might just be the ideal chance for a lasting peace agreement."[8]

Modi government is reasonably clear to deduce that the stress towards national security and defence in the 2019 elections cannot by itself ensure a third victory for PM Modi's Bhartiya Janata Party (BJP) in 2024. The economy will matter more and to boost the economy the requirement is fiscal responsibility, investment and structural reforms. This implies that the defence sector should not expect a cornucopia from Mr Modi. Rather there will be a tightening of strings, investment in using technology to improve efficiency, a few structural reforms and improving of the capability to influence the Indian Ocean region through the Indian Navy. With the same aim of strengthening defence, Modi will seek balancing alliances and greater capability to operate with partners in such alliances.

Defence Acquisitions

In the field of defence acquisitions PM Narendra Modi had learnt in a short time that this was a field where his conflicting interests of "Make in India" (his indigenisation mantra) and maintaining a high state of effectiveness were difficult to balance. While he has been clear in the importance to indigenous defence production in many security related forums and speeches, nevertheless, he has had to fast track several imported defence purchases through the 'government to government' route to speed up acquisition. These include the French Rafale aircraft; the US made M-777, A-2 ultra-light howitzers, Israeli Spike Anti-tank guided Missiles (ATGMs), and four guided missile frigates as well as S-400 Triumph Air Defence (AD) missiles from Russia. He may have reduced the number of units of an armament being purchased to balance financial resources. However, the deals can be open to acquire more units in the future or manufacture them within India. A clear realisation exists that indigenous defence industry will take time to pick up steam. Towards this end the slow moving Defence Research and Development Organisation (DRDO) and Ordnance factories are being goaded by the Modi government to deliver to face the axe. The government's concurrence to an army proposal for appointment of a serving army general as the manager of a factory which will produce the AK 203 rifle with Russian collaboration is one indicator.[9] In the past the Ordnance factories have been able to keep army officers out from senior managerial positions.

Appointment of Chief of Defence Staff (CDS)

Prime Minister Modi had sanctioned the undeniable requirement of a Chief of Defence Staff (CDS) to render single point military advice to the government. The requirement of Theatre Commands has also not materialised. However this is also because the three Services are as yet not in agreement among themselves in the utility of these reforms. The Indian Air Force advances strong arguments against having a CDS or Joint Theatre Commands. The government will have to push through these reforms much as the Nichols-Goldwater Act had pushed jointness in USA in the face of resistance by the Services.

National Security Strategy (NSS)

Another pending issue which defence analysts in India are awaiting from PM Modi is to have an articulated National Security Strategy (NSS). An NSS can set out political objectives for Indian military power as also the unclassified parts of it can enhance deterrence. The NSS can enable the fleshing out of the vision and roadmap for military, economic and intelligence development which will empower the nation to execute the defence strategy. It can only be hoped that the Modi government will see the writing of an NSS which will provide clear direction for strategic and operational options.

Conclusion

Defence reforms are normally desired but not implemented due to various internal and external influences. Historically, defence reforms come after catastrophic defeats or strategic surprises. In India, major reforms occurred after defeat in the 1962 war with China and the strategic surprise of the Kargil intrusions by Pakistan. In acquisition and organisation, the Defence reforms of the Modi government are nothing exceptional. Rather, they have raised hopes and then dropped them. The allocation of Rs 3.18 lakh crore for defence in the interim budget of February 2019 which remained unchanged when the budget was presented in July 2019 has been estimated at around 1.6 per cent of the GDP which, according to experts, is lowest since the 1962 war with China. So, no classic reforms have taken place involving enhanced financial outlays. This should not be a surprise because other than in times of war, the Central government, regardless of which party is in power has rightly balanced defence budgets with budgets for welfare, poverty alleviation and infrastructure development.

The reform that PM Modi can be credited with and which involves no financial outlay is in bringing in an offensive strategy in dealing with state sponsored acts of terrorism. This strategy can be called surprise, overt & declared, controlled retaliation. Colloquially this strategy is known in India as the strategy of "Surgical Strikes". It has been shouted hoarse by the opposition Congress party such actions have happened in the past also. The difference is that they were surprise, covert &undeclared, controlled retaliation. In current case, the strikes are overt, declared and the risk of escalation is higher. PM Modi took the decisive step of taking this risk. The Modi era will be remembered as one where for the first time Pakistan's nuclear bluff was called and escalation control was kept with India. However, this makes muscular responses the new normal which will put pressure on any future government to respond militarily to any outrage by Pakistan or its proxies.

The concept of the nested game theory propounded by the American political scientist George Tsebilis, is that in playing strategic games, actors are involved in several games at the same time and not only one game, and the strategic choices these actors makes in one game has implications for the other games they are involved in. Modi's critics say that the strategic game played post Pulwama by the air strike at Balakot was a nested game in which the choice of a "surgical strike" was made keeping in mind another ongoing game of the impending elections 40 days away. The decisive Mr Modi may have seized upon an opportunity, but the fact is, the national mood at that point of time was of justified intensive outrage, something had to be done. The positive of the action taken in the response to a terrorist attack which crossed the threshold was that it was firm and decisive. This has set a new benchmark. The deterrence it brings in will be validated in the future in case such attacks reoccur. However, it is undoubted that a degree of deterrence has been created. The proactive defence policy of PM Narendra Modi can justifiable and can be called his most visible defence reform.

Endnotes

1   PM's Address at the Combined Commander's Conference (2014). https://www.pmindia.gov.in/en/news_updates/pms-address-at-the-combined-commanders-conference/. Accessed on 2 July, 2021.

2   Press Information Bureau , Govt of India (2015). PM chairs Combined Commanders Conference on board INS Vikramaditya at Sea. http://pib.nic.in/newsite/PrintRelease.aspx?relid=133265. Accessed, 20 July, 2021.

3   Laxman. K. Behara. (2019). Defence Agenda for Modi Government 2.0. IDSA Policy Brief. https://idsa.in/policybrief/defence-agenda-modi-government-2.0-lkbehera-060619. Accessed, 22 July, 2021.

4   PM India News Updates. (2014). PM's address at the Combined Commanders Conference. https://www.pmindia.gov.in/en/news_updates/pms-address-at-the-combined-commanders-conference/. Accessed 24 July, 2021.

5   Hindustan Times,. (2015). As India conducts strikes in Myanmar, Pakistan warns against cross-border 'adventurism. https://www.hindustantimes.com/india/as-india-conducts-strikes-in-myanmar-pakistan-warns-against-cross-border-adventurism/story-MVDpQnyLW0V1VOWuh7iAhN.html. Accessed 26 July, 2021.

6   Rajesh Rajgopalan. (2016). India Now Controls the Escalation Debate. Raisiana Debates, ORF, https://www.orfonline.org/expert-speak/india-now-controls-the-escalation-ladder/. Accessed 27 July, 2021.

7   Sushant Sareen. (2019). Balakot air strikes: the end of the madman theory. https://www.orfonline.org/research/balakot-air-strikes-the-end-of-the-madman-theory-48730/. Accessed 28 July, 2021.

8   Hindol Sengupta. (2019). The Shisupala Doctrine: Narendra Modi and de-truncating the Indo-Pak power Asymmetry. https://www.orfonline.org/expert-speak/the-shishupala- doctrine-narendra-modi-de-truncating-indo-pak-power-asymmetry-51506/. Accessed 28 July, 2021.

9   Snehesh Alex Phillips. (2019). Army chief's new experiment — Major General is CEO of AK-203 rifle factory in Amethi. https://theprint.in/defence/army-chiefs-new-experiment-major- general-is-ceo-of-ak-203-rifle-factory-in-amethi/259019/. Accessed 29 July, 2021.

Section III

Perspectives from Indian Ocean and Indo-Pacific

Chapter 7

Significance of Andaman and Nicobar Islands in India's Maritime Strategy

Roshan Khanijo

Introduction

Historically, India's maritime trade has extended over thousands of years. In this journey, geography had played and still continues to play an important part in bolstering India's position as a significant power in the Indian Ocean Region (IOR). Traditionally, oceans have played a vital part in geo-economics and now with the gravitational pull shifting from Europe to Asia, the Indo-Pacific has become the new economic hub. According to Rear Admiral Alfred Mahan, an influential American geo-strategist, Indian Ocean plays a pivotal role: "Whoever controls the Indian Ocean dominates Asia. This ocean is the key to the seven seas, in the twenty-first century, the destiny of the world will be decided in these waters." Thus, this ocean will see a churning as nations compete and contest to maintain the balance of power. India on her part will remain a potent force when it comes to managing the affairs of this Ocean. The major reason being geographically the Indian peninsula juts into the India Ocean and fifty percent of the Indian Ocean basin lies within a 1,500 km radius of India, a reality that has strategic implications.[1] Further, India has 7516 km long coastline (including the coastline of Andaman and Nicobar Islands and Lakshadweep Islands) and has an Exclusive Economic Zone (EEZ) of an 2.37 million Sq. Km, which is the 12th largest EEZ in the world.[2] India has further filed two 'partial submissions' to United Nations Commission on the Limits of the Continental Shelf (CLCS) for the extension of the EEZ beyond 200 nautical miles, which could add approximately 1.2 million sq. km of extended Continental Shelf... thus India's sea bed –sub seabed area would become almost equal to its land area of 3.274 million sq.kms.[3] This is important because as stated by India's former diplomat and statesman, K M Panikkar "while to other countries, the Indian Ocean is only one of the important oceanic areas, to India it is a vital sea. Her life-lines are concentrated in that area, her freedom is dependent on the freedom of that water surface. No industrial development, no commercial growth, no stable political structure is possible for her unless her shores are protected"[4] Any hostile competition/conflict will adversely impact the growth and prosperity of this region. Hence, it is imperative that the transport corridors remain free, and for this security of the region becomes important. Thus, the economics and maritime security are intertwined and nations need to strengthen the latter to ensure freedom of navigation at high seas by not allowing the Sea Lanes of Communication (SLOCs) to be dominated by any one power; only then, unstinted economic growth is possible. This is especially relevant to the Indian Ocean Region (IOR) as the maritime environment of IOR is undergoing a transformation.

Strategic Environment in the IOR and India's Maritime Strategy

Since last few centuries, the Indian Ocean has seen an upswing both in terms of exploration of resources as well as activities of trade and commerce. This is because nearly forty percent of the world's offshore oil production takes place in the Indian Ocean basin also fishing, aquaculture, mineral resources and rare earths have made the blue economy an important determinant, as a result oceans have become an important conduit for trade and commerce - a key enabler for a nation's sustained growth yardstick. The volume of trade passing through the Indo-Pacific region has seen a steady growth, increasing the dependency of many nations on this ocean. The Indian Ocean is now the world's busiest trade route as more than 80 percent of the world's seaborne trade in oil (equivalent to about one-fifth of global energy supply) which fuels the economies of Southeast Asia, South Korea, Japan, and China—transits it.[5] India's economic growth has also made her more dependent on the sea. 95 percent of India's trade by volume and 68 percent of trade by value comes via the Indian Ocean.[6] Thus, freedom of navigation, safety and security of SLOCs and adhering to rules laid down by United Nations Convention on the Law of the Sea (UNCLOS) are essential indicators for smooth passage of trade and commerce. PM Modi during his keynote address at Shangri La Dialogue in 2018 (as attached in Appendix II) also highlighted that "common prosperity and security require us to evolve, through dialogue, a common rules-based order for the region, equal access as a right under international law to the use of common spaces on sea and in the air that would require freedom of navigation, unimpeded commerce and peaceful settlement of disputes in accordance with international law[7]".

This perception reflects a changed geo-political environment in IOR. With the relative decline of US and rise of China, a multi-polar world is more evident in Indo-Pacific region than anywhere else. The competition for resources is leading to security challenges. A significant factor is the presence of China in IOR. China through a well thought out maritime strategy is trying to change the status quo. China's economic alluring of small states by providing large financial assistance and the economic squeeze later on, due to non-payment of loans is impacting the economy of smaller nations. China's control of strategic assets mostly in the form of control of ports in IOR is enhancing its geo-strategic space. This has increased the number of Chinese bases in the IOR, providing Chinese Navy- logistic facilities, which has resulted in long and regular patrolling by Chinese ships and submarines in the IOR. This is transforming the security dynamics in the region.

Taking all these factors into consideration, the Indian maritime strategy includes a number of features. First and foremost, India needs to augment its maritime economy - which comprises a range of economic activities related to the maritime domain, including development of ports, coastal infrastructure, shipping, fishing, seaborne trade, offshore energy assets, undersea pipelines and cables, and seabed resources[8]. Secondly, due to this rise in the marine trade, India needs to collaborate with other nations' for securing the SLOCs, as transportation of marine cargo passing through these SLOCs and choke points is bound to increase and this will lead to security challenges. Thirdly, there has been blurring of lines as far as traditional and non-traditional threats are concerned, hence, India requires a holistic approach to maritime security. Dealing with maritime terrorism, piracy, trafficking/ smuggling, illegal, unreported and unregulated fishing (IUU), etc are some of the non-traditional threats. Also insurgencies, ethnic and civil wars, terrorism and prominence of non-state actors intensified by the spread of radical ideologies[9] have changed the nature of conflict. Similarly, there has been an increase in the number of ships and submarines of China and other extra regional powers patrolling the IOR, which is further impacting the status quo. India due to its geographical position and its strong navy can be a net security provider to littorals of IOR. Hence, amongst this entire conundrum, India needs to shape a favourable and positive maritime environment, for enhancing net security in India's areas of maritime interest.[10] Therefore, good friendly relations with the other littorals of the IOR are a larger politico-economic objective. Finally, climate change and natural disasters remain a constant source of worry for most of the littorals in the IOR and nations need to cooperate to tackle such threats.

Thus, 21st century security concerns are very different and therefore, the Indian Navy in 2015 has aptly revised its strategy as "Ensuring Secure Seas: Indian Maritime Security Strategy," which incorporates amongst others all the above mentioned factors. In this maritime strategy, Andaman and Nicobar Islands are bound to play a major role because of its geo-strategic location. Further, Andaman and Nicobar Islands are often called as an unsinkable aircraft carrier as they can perform the dual function of being India's outpost in the east as well as become an economic and tourist hub.

Geo-Strategic Importance of Andaman and Nicobar Islands

Geographically, Andaman and Nicobar Islands are situated 1200 km east of Indian mainland in the Bay of Bengal with a longitude of 92 to 94 degree east and latitude of 6 to 14 degree north. The two Island chain of Andaman and Nicobar are separated from each other by the 'Ten-degree Chanel' which is 150 degree wide and Andaman chain has nearly 550 islands of which only 28 are inhabited and Nicobar has some 22 main islands of which only 10 are inhabited.[11]The EEZ is 6 lakh sq. km and the biggest inhabited island is the Middle Andaman Island which has an area of 1536 sq. kms and the smallest inhabited island is Curlew Island which is just .03 sq. km.[12] Geo strategically, Andaman and Nicobar Islands are of utmost importance due to its proximity to the South East Asian nations' like Myanmar, Thailand, Malaysia, Indonesia (as shown in the map below) and also it is just 1092 km from Malacca Strait which is one of the busiest strait in the Indo-Pacific region, further it is 2477 km from Sunda and 3460 km from Lombok straits.

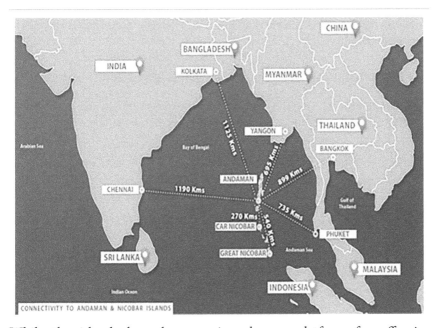

CONNECTIVITY TO ANDAMAN & NICOBAR ISLANDS

While the islands have been envisaged as a platform for offensive capabilities, their true benefit today lies in furthering maritime domain awareness and maintaining a naval advantage for India and its friends'.[13] For this it is essential that the infrastructure of the island is developed. Initially an Island Development Authority was formed in 1986 with Prime Minister as its Chairman to oversee the development of this region. However, due to tardy progress this was scrapped off and instead a new Island Development Agency (IDA) was formed in 2017, whereby Union Home Minister has been made the Chairman and Lieutenant Governor (LG) of Andaman and Nicobar Island is the executive head. By making a retired naval chief as the LG of the Union Territory, the government has showed its intention of developing Andaman & Nicobar Island on a fast track for both civil and military purposes. The LG now oversees conceptualisation, planning and execution of several big, strategic and development projects across the islands and the overarching purpose is to boost India's outreach to ASEAN countries as also the surveillance of the region for traditional and non-traditional threats.[14] The function of IDA is to guide the policies and programmes and guide the formulation of integrated master plans, review the policies, programmes, plan and their implementation for comprehensive development of islands and key areas for development have been identified. Final site potential development reports have been prepared for four Islands in Andaman & Nicobar namely Smith, Ross, Long and Aves Islands.[15]

Role of Andaman and Nicobar Island in India's Maritime Strategy

The Island's greatest asset is its proximity to South East Asia and to the major SLOCs of IOR, hence its major role would be to perform the dual function of strengthening India's relation with Association of the South East Asian Nations (ASEAN) through India's 'Act East Policy by projecting India's soft power and Secondly, they can become a springboard for India's maritime security strategy. India's policy of SAGAR which stands for Security and Growth for All in the Region, is a process to connect our Eastern region with the South East and East Asia. Under this India desires to boost its outreach to ASEAN countries, hence, government has plans to initiate direct trade and tourism between the islands and ASEAN countries especially direct flights between Port Blair and Phuket and Bangkok are on the anvil.[16] This is due to Andaman's proximity to these Islands as it takes just two hours to reach Bangkok and 1.5 hours for Phuket. Various ready to use eco-tourism resort projects are being planned and eco-tourism activities sensitive to the ecology, bio-diversity and the strategic locations of the islands are being promoted through this initiative.[17] The government is supporting not only tourism-based initiatives through single window-clearances and information system, but other integrated aspects related to physical and digital connectivity are also being addressed and the island administration is working in tandem with NITI Aayog on these initiatives.[18] The feasibility of trans-shipment terminal at South Bay, transhipment hub at Port Meadow along with developing better internal air connectivity linking Port Blair, Car Nicobar, Campbell Bay and Diglipur Airports to form an Air Circuit, as also Augmentation of satellite bandwidth from 3.2 GBPS in 2020 aggregate to 4 GBS by BSNL.

Trans-shipment terminal at Campbell Bay is especially of significance because large container ship can unload its cargo at this place instead of Maldives since Campbell is just 100 nautical miles from the Malacca strait. Further, mega tourism hubs are being planned so that major cruise liners can stop at these islands before they travel to Phuket/Singapore/Bangkok. The UDAN scheme will initiate first small commercial flights from and within the four airports of Port Blair, Car Nicobar, Campbell Bay and Diglipur and later on bigger projects can be planned. Along with this a better connectivity is also planned amongst these island chains and Andaman Trunk Road (ATR), Humphrey Strait Bridge, Roll-on/Roll-off Ferry Project and Improvement of Existing Jetty in Long Island are some projects being planned.[19] In the past due to lack of connectivity and poor surveillance of the islands especially Nicobar, there were instances where fisherman from neighbouring countries illegally visited these islands and disrupted marine wealth and forest. Further, due to radicalisation of neighbouring islands, these islands saw terrorists visiting and using it for poaching, arms, drug transhipments and such similar activities. However, now with the new initiative of creating better connectivity through air, road, bridges and improved jetties along with creation of tourist resorts, it would be possible to have better surveillance.

As far as, Indo-pacific is concerned, the centrality of Andaman Sea makes it an important asset for India. Whether it is the surveillance of major choke points or it is the power projection these Islands can be utilised optimally to achieve the said goal. Considering Andaman's northern part is just nearly 50 km from Myanmar's Coco Island and the southernmost point in Nicobar' Indira Point' is about 180 km from Aceh in Indonesia, it makes India along with other ASEAN countries a major stakeholder in the security of Malacca Straits. The seas at both the side of Malacca strait namely South China Sea and the Andaman Sea are vital to the smooth flow of global commerce. Historically, also the Andaman Sea was used by the Chola Empire, Maratha Admiral Kanhoji, and later on the Europeans to enhance the reach of their empires. In the past, these areas have been neglected as the development processes taken by the government had been very slow and intermittent, however with the Indo pacific becoming the new area for major power contestations, and especially the Chinese presence in this region, the government started rethinking and revamping its Andaman Nicobar policy.

China's economic rise, its modernisation of Navy and creation of maritime silk route to boost infrastructure development through control of littorals in the Indo-Pacific region and Africa has altered the balance of power in the region. China's legacy of offering large financial assistance to littorals is indirect method to enhance China's strategic space in the maritime domain. By supporting these states financially, China is also trying to take the control of strategic ports to be used for Chinese logistics. Kyaukypu, Hambantota, Gwadar, etc are some of the relevant examples. All these measures have increased the naval reach of China and this neo-colonialism is making the region more unstable, both in economic and security domain. Further, if China is successful in negotiating a deal with Thailand for the creation of Kra Canal, then, it will further raise China's power projection capabilities in the region. India's maritime interests require not only protection of India's sovereignty and territorial integrity against threats in the maritime environment, promote safety and security of Indian citizens, shipping, fishing, trade, energy supply, assets and resources in the maritime domain, but also pursue peace, stability and security in India's maritime zones, maritime neighbourhood and other areas of maritime interest.[20] This requires both, a nation's soft power as well as hard power.

Soon after the 1962 India-China war, the Indian Navy was made responsible for the defence of these islands, and in November 1962, a small garrison of 150 sailors was positioned at Port Blair, under a commander designated as Resident Naval Officer (RNO), however, over the years, the strength and status of this outpost grew progressively, and in 1976, the concept of a unified "Fortress Andaman and Nicobar" or Fortran was implemented under a Vice Admiral.[21] While the Army placed an infantry battalion and subsequently a brigade under the fortress commander, the IAF kept its units under one of the IAF commands, on the mainland with a liaison unit in the fortress Head Quarter.[22]

India in the past had disagreement about ownership of certain islands in the A&N islands with Myanmar; a bilateral maritime boundary agreement between the two countries saw the Coco island being ceded by India to Myanmar in 1987.[23] It has been alleged in the past that China had presence on this island. In October 2001, an Andaman and Nicobar Command was created and all other forces were put under this command which was to be headed by the C-in-C Andaman and Nicobar (CINCAN), and who reported to the Chairman COSC. The main aim of forming this command was to have greater jointness amongst all the three services and the coast guard for a smooth execution of its goals. Also, to have a better 'Maritime domain awareness' which "involves being cognizant of the position and intentions of all actors, whether own, hostile or neutral, and in all dimensions—on, over and under the seas."[24] The goals were all encompassing starting from "Defence of A&N Islands" including its waters, air space, humanitarian assistance and disaster relief (HADR), protection of future offshore installations, Coastal Security of ANI and rendering HADR to the littoral countries when required to Anti-poaching operations, prevention of human trafficking, illegal migration, smuggling, piracy, drug and gun trafficking.[25]

The non-traditional threats in the Andaman Islands have decreased due to constant surveillance of the navy, the coast guard and further backed by the army and air force units. Also defence diplomacy through Co-ordinated Patrols Exercise (CORPATs) with Myanmar, Indonesia and Thailand on a six monthly basis has been instrumental in achieving excellent synergy with the littoral navies.[26] Further, the biennial naval exercise 'MILAN' that started in 1995 with the participation of four nations has over the years grown and now there are over 15 countries participating in them. Though the command has grown as far as, its assets and powers are concerned, but the question remains if it has it developed in proportion to the role which it is supposed to play, considering that the geo-strategic environment prevailing is much more intense now than when the command was created in 2001.

The traditional threats from both the littorals as well as, extra regional powers are going to increase in the future. The number of Chinese ships and submarines patrolling the area has increased and this is because they have built logistics in the Indian Ocean littorals which enables them to sustain patrolling for longer durations. On the other hand, Pakistan has also increased the range of its missiles and is also developing its nuclear triad. It also plans to put dual use cruise missiles on its ships and submarines. Pakistan had also successfully tested Babur-3, a submarine-launched cruise missile (SLCM). In India also, there are proposed plans to enhance the resources with providing infrastructure to station a nuclear submarine and a Landing Platform Dock (LPD) along with a second Floating Dry Dock (FDN) and additional ships, also the Indian Air Force plans to position fighter aircraft in the islands along with increasing the number of operational airfields.[27] Resurfacing of runway at Air Force Station Car Nicobar, extension of runways at Campbell Bay and Shibpur are also planned, as also the number of naval vessels based in the island chain is planned for increase to 32.[28] India is also planning to conduct airborne radar surveys to map the surface topography of Andaman & Nicobar Islands which would help in better planning and response mechanisms against natural disasters.[29]

Challenges and Way Forward

The major challenge is the isolation of these Islands from the mainland and they being geographically dispersed which creates challenges as far as the surveillance and development of these islands are concerned. There are security concerns also since most of these islands are inhabited and hence are breeding grounds for transnational crimes, there have been instances in the past where citizens of other nations mainly, Myanmar and Thailand have approached these islands illegally for the purpose of poaching, drug and human trafficking and other such non-traditional threats. The only way forward is through better connectivity of these Islands with the mainland. This process has already started as more flights are being scheduled not only within India but with the neighbouring states also. As mentioned in earlier paragraphs, the government is trying to make Andaman and Nicobar a major tourist hub and this will increase the reach of the government to other smaller islands also. Government is also looking for developing eco-tourism on a public private partnership (PPP) basis and a conference was organised where potential investors, mostly from the hotel and tourism sectors, attended to explore the possibility of building tourist resorts, along with recreational and adventure sports facilities, in four islands in Andaman and Nicobar.[30] The internal security is also being strengthened as with development and connectivity government's reach will also increase and this will lead to better surveillance. The joint command of ANC is also trying to address this problem with greater patrolling and surveillance of these islands.

Secondly, there are environmental constrains as one has to be sensitive to the flora and fauna and tribal sensitivities. The availability of land for development, therefore, greatly decreases. Further, unequal development because of restrictions on protected areas has resulted in the focus of infrastructure at Port Blair only. Also, there is lack of telecommunication systems, poor land air and sea connectivity which impacts strategic and economic activities. Connectivity with the mainland and also inter-island connectivity with its relatively small population of around 3.80 lakh in ANI spread across many islands is required.

Government of India is addressing these issues and has started projects as mentioned earlier. One such project deliberated is the container transhipment terminal with the Free Trade Warehousing Zone in South Bay, Great Nicobar Island as government wants to utilise the natural depth (nearly 20 m) of Greater Nicobar can handle larger cargoes.[31] Though the government is addressing these issues, but it has to balance development with environmental concerns knowing the frailty of ecology. The 2004 Tsunami had damaged the Island when the jetties and runways were damaged. Thus, a strategy of encouraging and involving private sector, within the constraints of environmental and security issues, needs to be encouraged.[32]

Though the joint Command has been created but the capacity building both in terms of infrastructure and manpower is the responsibility of the individual services and often if there is a clash of interest, services may not give the same priority to ANC as may have warranted. The proof is that the assets of other services in ANC have not increased as much as was desired. In future the role of ANC is bound to increase hence, it is essential that planning and execution of policies should not be entangled in turf war and structures should be created for smooth execution of plans. Also it needs to be debated whether ANC should be made a full-fledged "theatre command".

Considering the security of Indo-Pacific has seen a rise of both traditional and non-traditional threats. Chinese activities have also grown in the eastern waters. There were alleged reports of them being involved in the Coco island. Their logistic support in the IOR has improved and there has been more patrolling of ships and submarines. In future, the waters of Indian Ocean are going to get more congested with conventional and nuclear assets and brinkmanship will increase. Also, there has been an increase in radicalisation of some of the littoral states the chances of these assets being acquired by the terrorists cannot be ruled out.

Thus, the challenges have increased. However, the location of these islands offers India a strategic view as they spread over the shipping lanes between the Gulf and the Malacca Straits that transport nearly 17 million tons of oil every day and hence, this strategic location makes them a corner stone in the Indian maritime strategy and requires upgradation of the Unified Andaman and Nicobar Command (UANC) into a potent deterrence force capable of taking on the threats.[33]

Conclusion

Government of India with the creation of Island Development Agency (IDA) has started giving due significance to these Islands. The process is underway with due cognizance being given to creating a balance between development, environment and security. The creation of a unified command in ANC is a step to mitigate both traditional and non-traditional threats. In this regard, the maritime strategy had articulated the 'Maritime Domain Awareness' (MDA) and by formulating policies and structures the ANC is trying to safeguard the maritime interest of the nation. Thus, a holistic process has started which includes not only *Ensures Secure Seas, and Shaping a Favourable and Positive Maritime Environment* but also protecting India's maritime interest by promoting safety and security of Indian citizens, shipping, fishing, trade, energy supply, assets and resources in the maritime domain.[34]

Endnotes

1   Harjeet Singh. (2009). India's Strategic Culture: The Impact of Geography. Manekshaw Paper. No 10. Center for Land Warfare Studies (CLAWS). KW Publishers Pvt Ltd. https://www.claws.in/images/publication_pdf/1249631214Manekshaw%20Paper%2010.pdf, Accessed 20 June, 2021.

2   Survey of the EEZ. National Center for Polar and Ocean Research (NCPOR). Ministry of Earth Sciences. Government of India. http://www.ncaor.gov.in/pages/researchview/7. Accessed 20 June, 2021.

3   Delimitations of the outer limits of the Continental Shelf. National Center for Polar and Ocean Research (NCPOR). Ministry of Earth Sciences. Government of India. http://www.ncaor.gov.in/pages/view/260/250-delineation-of-the-outer-limits-of-the-continental-shelf. Accessed 22 June, 2021.

4   K M Panikkar. (1946). India and the Indian Ocean. London: George Allen & Unwin. pp. 82-84.

5   John Lee Charles Horner. China Faces Barriers in the Indian Ocean, Hudson Institute. https://www.hudson.org/research/10054-china-faces-barriers-in-the-indian-ocean, Accessed 24 June, 2021.

6   Annual Report 2015-2016. Ministry of Shipping. Government of India. p. 4.

7   Prime Minister's Keynote Address at Shangri La Dialogue. (2018). Ministery of External Affairs.https://www.mea.gov.in/Speeches-Statements.htm?dtl/29943/Prime+Ministers+Keynote+Address+at+Shangri+La+Dialogue+June+01+2018

8   Ensuring Secure Sea: India's Maritime security Strategy (2015). Indian Navy Naval Strategic Publication (NSP). https://www.indiannavy.nic.in/sites/default/files/Indian_Maritime_Security_Strategy_Document_25Jan16.pdf. Accessed 26 June, 2021.

9   Bastien Irondelle. (2013). The New Parameters of International Security: Conceptual Introduction. https://www.iai.it/sites/default/files/TW_WP_13.pdf. Accessed June 27, 2021.

10 Ibid

11 Andaman and Nicobar Tourism Website. https://www.andamantourism.gov.in/html/andamans.html

12 Andaman and Nicobar Island at a Glance. https://web.archive.org/web/201606 05065940/http:// and ssw1.and.nic.in/ecostat/2015/glance/Ata Glance 2015.pdf

13 Darshana M Baraua. (2018). The Andaman and Nicobar Islands : India's Eastern Anchor in the Changing Indo-Pacific. https://warontherocks. com/2018/03/the-andaman-and-nicobar-islands-indias-eastern-anchor-in-a-changing-indo-pacific/. Accessed 26 June, 2021.

14 Nitin A Gokhlae. (2018). Andaman as Springboard for India's Act East Policy. Strategic News International. https://sniwire.com/defence-security/andamans-as-springboard-for-indias-act-east-policy/. Accessed 30 June, 2021.

15 Government of India. Ministry of Home Affairs. Lok Sabha Unstarred Question No. 3363. https://mha.gov.in/MHA1/Par2017/pdfs/par2018-pdfs/ls-07082018-English/3363.pdf. Accessed 30 June, 2021.

16 Nitin A Gokhlae. Op. Cit.

17 NITI Ayog. (2018). Incredible Islands of India Holistic Development. https://niti.gov.in/writereaddata/files/document_publication/IslandsDev. pdf. Accessed 30 June, 2021.

18 Ibid.

19 Ibid.

20 Ensuring Secure Sea: India's Maritime security Strategy. (2015). Op. Cit.

21 Vice Admiral Arun Prakash (Retd). PVSM, AVSM, VrC, VSM. (2003). Evolution of the Joint Andaman and Nicobar Command (ANC) and Defence of Our Island Territories (Part II). USI Journal. https://usiofindia. org/publication/usi-journal/evolution-of-the-joint-andaman-and-nicobar-command-anc-and-defence-of-our-island-territories-part-ii/. Accessed 30 June, 2021. Accessed 3 July, 2021.

22 Ibid.

23 Ibid.

24 Darshana M Baraua. (2018). Op. Cit.

25 Air Marshal PK Roy & Commodore A. Cawasji. (2017). Strategic Vision 2030: Security and Development of Andaman and Nicobar Islands. Vij Books Publication. New Delhi.

26 Denis Giles. (2015). Andaman and Nicobar Command to Celebrate its 15th Raising Day. http://www.andamanchronicle.net/index.php?option=com_content&view=article&id=7517:andaman-and-nicobar-command-to-celebrate-its-15th-raising-day&catid=37&Itemid=142. Accessed 3 July, 2021.

27   Air Marshal PK Roy & Commodore A. Cawasji. (2017). Op. Cit.

28   Ibid.

29   Livemint. (2021). Govt plans to conduct airborne radar surveys of Andaman & Nicobar Islands. https://www.livemint.com/news/india/govt-plans-to-conduct-airborne-radar-surveys-of-andaman-nicobar-islands-11628318770093.html, accessed March 13, 2022.

30   Sanjeeb Mukherjee. (2018). Govt plans to open up to 100 islands for eco-tourism in the next 12 months. Business Standard. https://www.business-standard.com/article/economy-policy/govt-plans-to-open-up-to-100-islands-for-eco-tourism-in-the-next-12-months-118081100059_1.html.

31   T.Raja Simhan. (2019). Transhipment Hub Planned in Andaman and Nicobar Island. Business line. https://www.thehindubusinessline.com/economy/logistics/transshipment-hub-planned-in-andaman-and-nicobar-islands/article28275263.ece. Accessed 5 July, 2021.

32   Speech by Deepak Mohanty.Executive Director. Reserve Bank of India., Delivered at Andaman Chamber of Commerce and Industry in Port Blair on 22 December 2011.

33   Air Marshal PK Roy & Commodore A. Cawasji. (2017). Op. Cit.

34   Ensuring Secure Sea: India's Maritime security Strategy. (2015). Op. Cit.

Chapter 7

India's Policy towards Indo-Pacific

Pankaj Jha

Introduction

In the last leg of his first term, Prime Minister Modi made a few pronouncements which were different from the usual approach he had taken in the initial years of his first term. He had said during the Shangri-La dialogue[1] in 2018 that Indo-Pacific need to be an all-inclusive construct whereby he had opened a window for China's engagement in this strategic construct (Prime Minister's Keynote Address at Shangri La Dialogue, 2018). However, after few months, he conducted the trilateral with United States (US) and Japanese leaders (Japan-US-India Summit Meeting, 2019)[2] and gave his consent to the concept of Quadrilateral Security Dialogue. In an overview, this looks counter–intuitive as these two measures appear opposite to one another. The first term left many unanswered questions about Modi' priorities and in the end of the first term, he engaged the Chinese President under the Wuhan spirit, making doors open for a possible rapprochement between the two Asian civilizations. During the same time, with United States (US), the issue of tariffs and visa limitations to Indians was playing in the minds of the analysts and observers and a few academics made pronouncements that the congenial period between India and US has ended. Further, the regular meetings continued with Russia and China while at the same time, courting US and Japan on the sidelines of the G-20 summits. The question arises whether India wants a multi-alignment at its own terms without ceding its strategic autonomy to the cajoling by the US and China. The first term of PM Modi inherited a few challenges also which included the looming international recession because of US-China trade war, tensions between US and Iran, Japan and Korea frictions and the problems related to the different theatres in Asia–Pacific which included Chinese navy exercises closer to the Australia coast, China's assertive posture in South China Sea including in those areas which were non-contentious and the island building in the South China Sea along with deployment of strategic missiles.

The second term of Prime Minister Modi that began in 2019 came with a lot of questions regarding his domestic priorities and international commitments. However, while the first term saw multiple meetings in the initial two months starting with Nepal, Bhutan, Sri Lanka, the second term saw the visits to Maldives and Bhutan within the first three months of his second term. Modi has been weighing the options and looking to engage the major powers through his deft diplomatic initiatives. The elevation of S Jaishankar (former foreign secretary) as the new foreign minister clearly outlined his outcome-based and specialized approach to foreign policy objectives. Jaishankar, being a seasoned diplomat who had worked as India's Ambassador to both US and China, clearly knows the task that was expected of him. Further, the institution of the Indo-Pacific division (Thakkar, 2019)[3] in the Indian foreign ministry objectifies the role that Indo-pacific is going to play in India's larger foreign policy discourse.

Prime Minister Modi in his first speech made in the Parliament made it clear that he wants accelerated growth and also better economic management. He said that there should be less governance but the governance is always there where there is lack of it. In his oath taking ceremony in 2019, he extended invitation to the Bay of Bengal Initiative for Multi-Sectoral Technical and Economic Cooperation (BIMSTEC) countries, (India Today, 2019)[4] which clearly means building a connect between the immediate and extended neighbourhood. Further, BIMSTEC is thought of as a process which is unexplored despite immense potential. The important agendas for Modi in his second term are to initiate dialogue with technology sufficient countries such as Japan, Germany and Israel, in a more collaborative way, so as to promote Made in India and also working on joint ventures. Modi has stated that Japan would remain an important partner for India (India Today, 2019b)[5] and similar expression was used in the case of South Korea and also Australia. Modi had undertaken the FIPIC (Forum for India-Pacific Island Cooperation) initiative and two summit level meetings have already taken place while more interactions have been initiated with the island countries located in the Oceania region in the fields of health diplomacy, climate change, sustainable development, blue economy and also working in small technology initiatives and skill development in these island countries. Modi has made it clear that trade and export led promotion would be important elements for the growth of the country. This sentiment was reflected in his Independence Day speech in 2019 where he asked the provinces and districts to identify their niche areas and identify select products which can be used for exports.

Indo-Pacific region would mean India should be included in the Asia-Pacific Architecture through institutional arrangements such as Asia Pacific Economic Cooperation (APEC), Pacific Island Forum (PIF) and working with regard to many other institutional arrangements at Track 1.5 and Track II. The issue that would challenge the Indian Foreign policy would be to bring synergies between the Indo-Pacific, Asia-Pacific and the Indian Ocean region.

Addressing Challenges in the Indo-Pacific

During the Shangri-La dialogue in 2018, PM Modi proposed that the Indo-Pacific should not be an exclusive regional construct instead it should be an inclusive club. However, immediately upon his return, he instated a new division, known as Indo-Pacific in the Ministry of External Affairs in 2019. The Wuhan and Mamallapuram informal dialogues with President Xi failed to produce anything substantial between India and China as the tangible movement in terms of border issue and the differences with regard to the trade imbalance continued. On the other hand, differences of opinion with the US have been there in terms of the geographical definition of the Indo-Pacific and America's unhappiness with India ties with Iran and Russia. The Quad initiative (India, Japan, the US and Australia) has taken off after China's decision to use border dispute as a leverage against India's close relationship with the US and other Quad members. However, India would not want Quad to turn into a military alliance and Biden administration's decision to supply nuclear submarine technology to Australia under the newly formed alliance, AUKUS points to the fact that Quad would not go the military alliance way.

While Association of South East Asian Nations (ASEAN) has its own share of problems with the Indo-Pacific construct (ASEAN Outlook on the Indo-

Pacific, 2019)[6] and has to hold a meeting synergizing ASEAN priorities and objectives with the larger trans-regional imagination. The promise of the 'Code of Conduct', also showed signs but the recurrent display of power projection by China has brought the issue to the brink of a military skirmish between the claimant nations and China. The South China Sea has invariably become the epicenter of power politics with China regularly threatening the legitimate exploration rights of Vietnam in the Exclusive Economic Zone (EEZ). The response from the international community has not been very encouraging and military confrontation could breakout in this area.

ASEAN as an institution has been grappling with the concept of Indo-Pacific and the threat loomed large in the multilateral organizations psyche that Indo-Pacific would subsume the ASEAN in its fold. The issue of centrality of ASEAN would be compromised within the larger discourse of regional security and major power struggle given the fact that Beijing has been flexing its muscles in the 'near abroad'. Countries such as Singapore have chosen to remain neutral to the Indo-Pacific concept while other claimant nations such as Philippines and Vietnam incrementally subscribing to the concept. Indonesia is getting more active to regain control of ASEAN which it had ceded to Singapore in late 1990s when it faced political instability and the plummeting Rupiah (Indonesian Currency). The issue is the countries such as Indonesia and Australia desire that Indo-Pacific should act as a guarantor against Chinese adventurism and even the Quad and AUKUS could be looking to tailor their role in the regional security apparatus. How and in which way this would be achieved is being planned and the blueprint is still not ready.

The Challenge of Regional Economic Institutions

During his oath-taking ceremony in 2019, PM Modi had invited the heads of government/state of BIMSTEC countries, clearly outlining that the first connect with the Indo-Pacific would come through the BIMSTEC route. However, the problem has been exploring the potential and possibilities with regard to BIMSTEC. India has undertaken the transnational transport initiative known as BBIN (Bangladesh, Bhutan, India, Nepal). The issues that still need to be addressed are the fitness of the vehicles, license of the transporters and also driver's license which should be entertained and accepted at the borders of the BBIN countries. Another important aspect is ensuring that contraband and weapons should not be couriered through these trade routes. Also customs process and integrated posts for quick clearance of the cargo are to be addressed. While Bangladesh, Bhutan, India, Nepal (BBIN) has shown promise when cargo from Nepal was transported to the Bangladesh and Indian ports for further exports, Bhutan has stringent laws with regard to strict pollution compliance and therefore, there is a need for a certain category of vehicle which need to be cleared for pollution certificate. Bhutan's upper house has not yet ratified the BBIN pact and has decided to stay out of the sub-regional connectivity plan for the time being.

In the context of BBIN, it has been proposed that it can be expanded to the countries like Myanmar and Thailand, so that it seamlessly integrates with the BIMSTEC agenda of transport and trade promotion and also facilitate people to people (P2P) contacts through these land routes. The India-Myanmar-Thailand Trilateral highway is not yet fully operational. There are two streams of thoughts which are being proposed in this, transport and infrastructure corridor. The first one proposes that integrating BIMSTEC, Mekong-India Economic Corridor (MIEC) would serve India's interest while the second one stresses on strengthening Indo-Pacific Economic Corridor (IPEC)with US assistance integrating these economic regions in one common economic network. Few scholars have proposed that BIMSTEC should be expanded to include other countries such as Vietnam in this process. PM Modi has been a strong supporter of the vision of former PM Atal Bihari Vajpayee and he has proposed that there should be road and railway network from Delhi to Hanoi (Vietnam). PM Modi would be willing to work towards this dream of his political mentor. Also, the Mekong India Economic Corridor needs more infusion of funds and institutional support to integrate India's production network with that of mainland Southeast Asia. The regional value chain has not seen integration of India in the export oriented economies of Southeast Asia. This might be the agenda for the Modi government in coming years as it would like that with economic impetus and support, the eastern parts of India should get necessary economic incentives to get integrated with the Southeast Asian markets. This is also the focus of India's Act East policy and the Supply Chain Resilience Initiative (SCRI) that would seek sustainable, balanced and inclusive growth in the Indo-Pacific.

The production costs of China and the US-China trade war has imposed certain benefits to low cost production economies, and India looks to gain from this trade war. India is also looking to benefit from the fact that many countries want to divert their supply chains from China after the COVID-19 pandemic and want to avoid overdependence on Beijing in trade matters. However, the challenge is to get necessary infrastructure and better bureaucratic structures to support accelerated growth and Foreign Direct Investment. While many institutional changes have been brought about which includes the abrogation of the Foreign Investment Promotion Board (FIPB) and easy access to investment in certain sectors and even allowing 100 per cent Foreign Direct Investment (FDI) in select sectors. However, PM Modi would have to work to addressing root causes of civil unrest and the snit-reform mindset which impacts the foreign investors' confidence. PM Modi has addressed the ease of business at multiple levels and has brought about structural change through integrated tax structures and also imposing Goods and Service tax (GST) which might be good for the economy in the long run but structural changes have not kept up with the changes in the tax structures leading to job losses and also redundancy of many industrial units which were family managed or have less than twenty workers. The costs of compliance and penalties for non-compliance and on reporting of taxes have further reduced the confidence of the domestic investors and entrepreneurs. With global economy on a down slide after the Corona pandemic, the channels to infuse the economic growth in such circumstances would be a major challenge for the National Democratic Alliance (NDA) government.

For India the challenge would be to explore avenues to promote economic growth and trade. India has already opted out of the Regional Comprehensive Economic Partnership (RCEP) and would have to look for other avenues like bilateral free trade agreements with EU, the US, the UK, Australia, South Korea and others to protect its trade interests. Given India's trade deficit in the ASEAN FTA, it is likely to be renegotiated. In his first term, PM Modi had proposed that it would work in terms of Security and Growth for All in the Region (SAGAR). The first term of Modi proposed extensive infrastructure network Sagarmala (String for Oceans) encompassing highway and port network, Golden Quadrilateral highway network, river linking plan to promote inland waterways, and sub-regional initiatives through India-Thailand- Myanmar Trilateral Highway network to further integrate Southern Asian economies. Indian economy is coming out of the COVID-19 slump and as per the estimates of International Monetary Fund, it is expected to grow at 9.5 percent in the year 2021 and 8.5 percent in 2022. India's economic growth prospects have the potential to benefit not only its own population but also the regional economies.

For Prime Minister Modi the priority would also be to strongly propose India's candidature of APEC. Since 1994 India has requested for the membership of APEC and the then Indian Prime Minister P.V. Narasimha Rao referring to India's inclusion in APEC stated, "I don't want to knock on closed doors" (Pereira, 1994)[7]. In response to this, Singapore Prime Minister Goh Chok said "the doors may be closed but are not locked". However, in 1996, the then Singapore Foreign Minister S Jayakumar accepted, "it would be hard to imagine an Asia-Pacific century without India's participation" (APEC 2015)[8]. Even after the moratorium on new membership was over in 2010, India's candidature at the forum needs strong support where it has been an observer since 2011. In support of its membership to the APEC, India meets the five prerequisites, that is firstly, it is located within the Asia-Pacific. Secondly it has expansive economic ties (India's trade has been relatively high) with the APEC economies. Thirdly, it has incrementally transformed into a market oriented economy and adopted free trade policy. Fourthly, it absorbed multiple economic parameters as per the APEC criteria; and lastly, for meeting membership criteria India has shown commitment to adopt an individual plan of action and assimilate APEC's programmes with focused approach. However, 'the bigger question is whether India is prepared for the APEC futuristic rules, business facilitation processes, and digitized procedures since it has recently walked out of the RCEP. However, India needs to work on the tariff regime and also for reducing non-tariff barriers in a phased manner (Star and Jha, 2019)[9]. Not only economic challenges, India will have to look into strategic and geo-political challenges as well in the Indo-Pacific region.

Challenges in the Indo-Pacific

The major challenge that India faces in the Indo–Pacific would be related to the increasing assertive China and the island building activities as well as, deployment of missiles in those islands and its attempts to counter India's military influence in the Indian Ocean Region. China has started encroaching in other strategic spaces including the Block 0.6 which has been explored jointly by Russia, India and Vietnam and lies closer to the Vietnam EEZ. The increasing Chinese aggressive posture would mean a disturbed region impacting India's trade and commerce and also impeding the freedom of navigation. The role that India needs to play would have long term effects on its relations with the major powers in the region as well as, protecting its own interests. US has been cajoling North Korea but given its overextensions in multiple theaters – in Syria, Iran, Latin America and also in South China Sea, the listing of priorities would be difficult and also depends on the best scenario. The US engagement with Iran would mean that US influence in East Asia would reduce while at the same time China's threatening posture without any military guarantee from the US would mean that US allies would start looking for their options. The US has not initiated countermoves against Chinese influence in Southeast Asia and the support initiatives. Further, China's inroads in the Indian Ocean particularly in Maldives, Malaysia and Indonesia would be of concern to PM Modi. Also China has been building an aid and assistance network in Papua New Guinea, Timor Leste and Vanuatu thereby, taking the power struggle between different powers to the Indo-Pacific region particularly in Oceania. With the developments in the Indo-Pacific region and more subscribers to the China's Belt and Road initiative as well as, maritime projects of port development in Sihanoukville, Indonesia (two port development projects) and in Timor (development of coastal highways). India would be seeking to develop intricate network of exercises, coordinated patrol with countries such as Australia and Indonesia as well as developing its Andaman and Nicobar command. During the Independence day speech in 2019, PM Modi approved the establishment of the Chief of Defence Staff (CDS), (Indian Today, 2019c)[10] who would look for interoperability and acquisitions which should develop jointmanship instead of intra services rivalry. India will also have to work on counter-terrorism initiatives and build its own network of convenient infrastructure in collaboration with willing countries such as the Quad partners and Indonesia. The proposed development of Sabang port in Indonesia and also satellite networks for the friendly countries would be on agenda for India in coming months. A number of countries such as Vietnam, Indonesia and Thailand have requested India for the export of Brahmos missiles and India would have to work for a comprehensive plan for promoting India's defence exports to the countries of Indo-Pacific and build official network through liaison visits and training of personnel. India would be promoting 'Make in India',

Initiative more vigorously and in this context, Indo–Pacific nations would be a priority particularly those which have been charmed by the cheap Chinese military exports.

Conclusion

India will be facing strategic and economic challenges in its Indo-Pacific policy. India wants to sustain and promote its Make in India initiatives and would have to take hard decisions with regard to tariff reductions and make itself ready for the next set of reforms which have been set in motion by the implementation of digital payment systems, universal banking and also the goods and services tax (GST). The unstable global security situation, particularly with regard to Corona induced slumps, turbulence in stock markets and financial liquidity crisis would mean that India would have to tread cautiously. On the strategic front, greater engagement for economic benefits and developing defense cooperative structures would help India in the short term. More economic and strategic collaboration with like-minded countries like the Quad partners will exist. The strengthening of sub-regional economic initiatives would be the agenda for India. One can say with conviction that India would be marred with more strategic and economic challenges in the Indo-Pacific with limited choices.

Endnotes

1   Prime Minister's Keynote Address at Shangri La Dialogue. (2018). https://www.mea.gov.in/Speeches-Statements.htm?dtl/29943/Prime+Ministers+Keynote+Address+at+Shangri+La+Dialogue+June+01+2018/.Accessed on 25 August 2019.

2   Japan-U.S.-India Summit Meeting. (2019). https://www.mofa.go.jp/s_sa/sw/page3e_001038.html/. Accessed on 25 August 2019.

3   Thakkar, Aman. (2019). 5 Big Ideas for the Indian Foreign Ministry's New Indo-Pacific Desk. https://thediplomat.com/2019/05/5-big-ideas-for-the-indian-foreign-ministrys-new-indo-pacific-desk/. Accessed on 22 August 2019.

4   India Today. (2019). BIMSTEC leaders reach Delhi for PM Narendra Modi's oath-taking ceremony. May 30. https://www.indiatoday.in/india/story/bimstec-leaders-in-delhi-to-attend-aoth-taking-ceremony-of-pm-modi-1538519-2019-05-30. Accessed on 25 August 2019.

5   India Today. (2019b). Japan played an important role in India's economic development: PM Narendra Modi. June 27. https://www.indiatoday.in/india/story/narendra-modi-japan-india-economic-development-1557361-2019-06-27. Accessed on 22 August 2019.

6   ASEAN Outlook on the Indo-Pacific. (2019). https://asean.org/storage/2019/06/ASEAN-Outlook-on-the-Indo-Pacific_FINAL_22062019.pdf/. Accessed on 25 August 2019.

7   Pereira, Derwin. (1994). PM Goh happy that Rao has raised 'Indian fever'. September 10. http://derwinpereiramedia.com/derwin-pereira-pm-goh-happy-that-rao-has-raised-indian-fever/. Accessed on 22 August 2019.

8   APEC. (2015) Building Inclusive Economies, building a Better World. http://apec2015.ph/ apec-2015//. Accessed on 3 June 2019.

9   Star, Shaun and Pankaj Jha. (2019). An Australian perspective. https://perthusasia.edu.au/getattachment/Our-Work/India-in-APEC-Views-from-the-Indo-Pacific/PerthUSAsiaCentre-India-in-APEC.pdf.aspx?lang=en-AU/. Accessed on 22 August 2019.

10 India Today. (2019c). PM Narendra Modi's mega announcement: India will now have Chief of Defence Staff. 15 August. https://www.indiatoday.in/india/story/pm-narendra-modi-announces-chief-of-defence-staff-independence-day-speech-1581006-2019-08-15. Accessed on 22 August 2019.

Chapter 9

Role of Andaman and Nicobar Islands as a Maritime Strategic Hub

Raj Kumar Sharma

Introduction

India is strategically located as a continental and maritime power in the Indian Ocean Region (IOR). India thinks beyond the Westphalian notion of political borders and treats the Indian Ocean as a cultural space where Indian culture has influenced other cultures. The IOR influences other countries while it is India which has influenced the IOR throughout history. During British times, the British ruled from the Gulf of Aden to Singapore and the Indian rupee was used as a currency in this area. That is why; India cannot restrict itself to political boundaries in IOR and sees the ocean as its sphere of influence.[1] After India's independence, its strategic focus has been on land borders as New Delhi has border disputes with Pakistan and China. During the Cold War, India argued for a zone of peace in the IOR where the US and Soviet Union were vying for influence. India's engagement with the IOR countries began to rise after 1991, as New Delhi liberalised its economy and maritime trade started to pick up. In the contemporary context, India seeks to shape the emerging security architecture in the IOR through initiatives like Indian Ocean Naval Symposium (IONS), Indian Ocean Rim Association (IORA), Bay of Bengal Initiative for Multi-Sectoral Technical and Economic Cooperation (BIMSTEC), Mekong Ganga Cooperation (MGC), Quadrilateral Security Dialogue, Indian Ocean Dialogue, efforts to build maritime domain awareness and strengthening the military potential of the Andaman and Nicobar Islands (ANI).

In the current geopolitical context, IOR is witnessing strategic contestation with extra-regional and regional powers trying to safeguard their national interests. From India's perspective, China's rise in the IOR comes as a strategic challenge as India-China relations suffer from strategic mistrust and the two Asian giants are still to solve their land border dispute in the high Himalayas. Eighty percent of China's oil imports and most of its trade with Africa, West Asia and Europe pass through the IOR. Majority of India's trade and energy also transits through the IOR, which makes it important for India's economic and energy security. With rising economic and maritime capabilities, India is interested in shaping the strategic environment in the IOR, unlike the Cold War days when India had limited capabilities and a continental focus. India sees IOR as its sphere of influence and presence of an adversarial power could impact Indian security and economic interests. India aims to be the net security provider in the IOR. According to Indian Maritime Security Strategy Document 2016, net security is *"the state of actual security available in an area, upon balancing prevailing threats, inherent risks and rising challenges in a maritime environment, against the ability to monitor, contain and counter all of these."*

India is the only regional country with required naval capabilities in IOR to take up the role of net security provider. Prime Minister Narendra Modi in 2015 had said that India's vision for IOR is inherent in the concept of SAGAR (a Hindi word that means sea), which stands for "Security and Growth for All in the Region". This policy has four main pillars. *One*, India desires to be the net security provider in IOR. *Two*, there will be active diplomatic engagement with friendly countries and relevant stakeholders in the IOR. India would assist the regional countries to build their maritime capacities and economic strengths including areas like sustainable development and blue economy. *Three*, India would work to develop agencies for collective action for peace and security in the IOR. *Four*, the main responsibility for peace, stability and prosperity in the IOR would be with the regional countries, not the extra-regional power.[2]

In the IOR, India has two strategic advantages – Lakshadweep and Minicoy Islands on its western flank and the Andaman and Nicobar Islands on eastern flank which extend India's maritime reach in IOR. Given their strategic location and potential, there is special place for ANI in India's maritime strategy. Aspects of ANI as a maritime strategic hub in India's IOR strategy are explained in succeeding paragraphs based on primary sources. Interviews have been conducted with experts who have served Indian defence forces and are now engaged in research on foreign and security issues of India.

ANI as a Strategic Maritime Hub

Andaman and Nicobar Islands is also called India's 'unsinkable aircraft carrier' in the Bay of Bengal. Out of the total 572 islands, only 38 are inhabited, comprise 30 per cent of India's Exclusive Economic Zone (EEZ). They are important for the sea lanes of communication (SLOCs) and due to their location at the intersection of the Indian Ocean and the South China Sea, and further to the Pacific Ocean, ANI is an important fulcrum of the strategic concept of the Indo-Pacific, as depicted in map below.[3]

Strategic Location of the Andaman and Nicobar Islands

Source: The Little People of the Andaman Islands

ANI as a strategic maritime hub means the island has economic and security potential and India should try to tap into it.[4] ANI can be considered as the easternmost outpost of India strategically located in the Bay of Bengal and Andaman Sea. What makes it special is the proximity to the Straits of Malacca and Singapore (SOMS) from where the entire area can be kept under surveillance. Important Sea Lanes of Communication (SLOCs) can be monitored from ANI. The traffic through the SOMS is crucial for energy security, trade and also for sustaining the economic growth of the countries on either side of SOMS. For China as well as for India, the straits are crucial for unimpeded movement of trade and energy.[5] The international ships that pass through the region need transhipping ports and trade hubs which are close to main shipping channels. That is why; India has also started cargo shipping facility at Campbell Bay in ANI. India is also emerging as maritime domain awareness (MDA) hub in IOR where it is collecting and distributing information to friendly countries. The Indian Navy has an information fusion centre in Gurugram which sees participation of many regional and extra-regional navies.

The island is also important from the perspective of non-traditional security to check activities like piracy, armed robbery, trafficking etc. Indian Navy's biennial exercises, Multilateral Navel Exercises (MILAN) are held at Port Blair where countries from Southeast Asia also participate and their focus is on humanitarian relief and non-combatant evacuation drills. To justify its 'security provider' status, the Indian Navy realises the need to maintain necessary force levels on the islands.[6] ANI is also important for forewarning of storms and Tsunamis as it hits this region before hitting the mainland and hence allows for a better response from the coastal states in India and also the neighbouring state.[7] Economically, ANI gives a huge Exclusive Economic Zone (EEZ) to India which mainly has a benefit of fisheries but there is a potential for hydrocarbons as well in future. From tourism, fisheries, sea bed mining to offshore hydrocarbons, there is lot that can be done around ANI.[8]

Despite having immense economic and security potential, development of ANI has been at a slow pace. Keeping in view its long-term maritime security interests, India established its first and only Tri-Service Command at ANI in 2001. A number of factors hinder development efforts towards ANI. According to Commodore Somen Banerjee, senior fellow at Vivekananda International Foundation, in New Delhi, development of any area is a process which is influenced by domestic factors. India always had the intent to develop ANI but there was lack of funding sources. Since now Indian economy is on the rise, there is potential to develop these islands as a strategic hub. Commodore Abhay K Singh from Manohar Parrikar Institute for Defence Studies and Analyses (MP-IDSA) has further pointed out that there has been a dilemma for Indian policymakers – should they tap economy or strategic aspects of ANI first, as both lead to different conclusions. Abhijit Singh from Observer Research Foundation

(ORF) opined that in India, a section of foreign policy experts has been against development of military infrastructure on the island as this could be seen with suspicion in Southeast Asian countries that see India as a benign power. Indonesia and Malaysia in particular did not see this as a good development in the past. However, he highlighted that since China's presence in South Asia and IOR started to push India on defensive in its own backyard, India had to develop ANI as a strategic hub. As pointed out earlier, ANI can also play an important role in humanitarian assistance and disaster relief not only for India but also the Southeast Asian nations. Countries like Vietnam and Singapore support India's military presence at ANI while India's deepening maritime security cooperation between Indonesia and Malaysia hints that they now support such efforts by India. India, Singapore and Thailand have started to hold naval exercise, STIMEX in the Andaman Sea, a sign of strategic significance of ANI in India's growing security cooperation with Southeast Asian nations. These countries realise that India can be a balancer to China in their maritime disputes with Beijing and in this regard, India's efforts to have more military presence at ANI would eventually benefit them. India and Indonesia are jointly developing the deep sea port of Sabang in Indonesia which is just 19 nautical miles away from ANI. ASEAN's view of Indo-Pacific is close to that of India, emphasising on respect for sovereignty, international law and peaceful settlement of disputes.

Andaman and Nicobar Island and China Factor in IOR

From India's maritime security perspective, it is the rise of China in waters around India that has raised eyebrows in New Delhi's strategic circles. Given their border dispute, India is treading a cautious path vis-a-vis China, a country whose strategic culture is highlighted by deception and stratagem. Under its 'Two-Ocean' strategy, Beijing has plans to dominate the Pacific and Indian Ocean. China's grand vision of Maritime Silk Road (MSR) under the Belt and Road Initiative, its need to protect its trade and energy supplies passing through IOR to overcome its Malacca Dilemma and reasons like anti-piracy operations around the Gulf of Aden offer China a pretext to deploy naval assets in the IOR. The presence of PLA Navy units in IOR started more than a decade ago when Chinese naval ships were deployed for anti-piracy missions. This has allowed them to get an excellent idea of the environment not just along the African coast but in the Indian Ocean and have added to the database of the environment, sea conditions, weather, shipping and an opportunity for evaluation of the peacetime deployment of navies in the region. The routine deployment of both conventional and nuclear submarines is indicative of China's desire to emerge as a power of consequence in IOR. The trends suggest at militarisation of IOR as China's first overseas military base has come up at Djibouti while it is now an open secret that they have strong military presence at Gwadar. There have been media reports in India about entry of Chinese ships in India's EEZ without seeking permission from India. China's close interaction with Pakistan, an all-weather ally could allow Beijing to intervene on its behalf in times of crisis in the North Arabian Sea where Indian Naval units have enjoyed superiority. The commercial investments in the ports of Bay of Bengal rim nations and military engagement by way of supply of naval ships and weapon systems provide an opportunity for China to be relevant in the maritime equations in the Bay of Bengal.[9]

Given its strategic location in the IOR, India is in commanding position as it controls the internal lines of connectivity to the ocean while China is trying to build such internal lines through initiatives like China Pakistan Economic Corridor (CPEC) to gain control in IOR. If the Chinese military modernisation goes as per their plans, they will have a two ocean navy by 2035. They will have six aircraft carriers including four nuclear by 2035. India is hard pressed to match up to China's IOR plans.[10] For India, ANI acts as a static aircraft carrier which would help in dealing with China's rising profile in IOR. The Tri Services Command (TSC) at ANI provides the optimum C4ISR (Command, Control, Communications, Computer, Intelligence, Surveillance, and Reconnaissance) capability to ensure that there are no surprises when the Chinese vessels enter the Indian Ocean in pursuit of their missions.

The combined might of Indian Navy, Air Force and the Army will ensure that they are in a position to thwart any advance of Peoples Liberation Army (PLA) Navy forces in times of hostilities with Pakistan or any other situation requiring forward posturing and presence.[11] Surveillance purpose of ANI can help in protecting Indian assets in South China Sea like oil fields that are part of India-Vietnam agreement. As India gets access to Cam Ranh Bay in Vietnam, Sabang deep sea port in Indonesia and Changi naval base in Singapore, there will be an important role for ANI in this regard.[12] India does not maintain heavy military presence at ANI since the distance between mainland India and the island is not too much, unlike the case between the US and Hawaii. When a threat develops, assets can be shifted to ANI. In case of hostilities with China, India can declare a blockade or Maritime Exclusion Zone around the Malacca Straits and the ANI will play a critical role in such circumstances. China has been using coercion, compellence and deterrence against India in peacetime to influence foreign policy of IOR states. ANI will be important to shape the diplomatic and strategic space in IOR for India. India wants to be a net security provider in IOR through intelligence gathering, capacity building, maritime domain awareness, white shipping agreements etc. Shaping leads to power projection and ANI has potential in this regard. China is not able to do maritime reconnaissance in IOR as it does not have an airfield in the region. India has stationed Poseidon-8I maritime reconnaissance aircrafts at ANI to monitor China's strategic movement in IOR, thus giving an edge to India. India plans to have more maritime reconnaissance aircrafts on ANI in future.[13] India's security efforts in IOR would be further boosted by improved surveillance facilities, and naval assets like warships positioned on strategic nodes at the ANI.[14] Two developments may further push India to upgrade its military presence at the ANI. *First*, China's potential plans to build a Kra canal cutting across isthmus of Thailand to reduce its dependence on the Malacca Straits. There are many barriers to this project and China may not have made up its mind fully about it. *Second*, news reports indicate that China is building a military base in Cambodia, 1,200 km away from ANI. Both these developments will bring focus back on the strategic potential of ANI and force India to upgrade its military presence on these islands. India may plan eventually to have a permanent fleet at the ANI, making it important in India's sea denial strategy against China in the IOR. India and the other Quad countries, the US, Japan and Australia may install sound surveillance sensors in the vicinity of ANI to monitor China's activities.[15] The ANI also has an important role in any attempt for collaborative effort towards anti-submarine warfare between the Quad countries.[16]

India's Policy towards ANI

Under Prime Minister Narendra Modi, India is making efforts to better integrate the islands with India through their sustainable development. The blue economy initiatives (BEI) will be the guiding principle for developing ANI. Under the Act East policy, India has further intensified its engagement with Southeast Asian countries. The visible difference is in fast-tracking the processes and ensuring that the nation is ready to face any challenges in its area of interest.[17] Modi governments approach is to take one step at a time. The current focus is on building infrastructure on the islands and to develop the tourism industry. The overall focus is to develop ANI into a smart island. The government has pro-active planning and is pursuing connectivity between ASEAN and ANI. It is trying to build economic interdependence between the two. India should also try to connect BIMSTEC with ASEAN as a pilot project.[18] ASEAN's outlook on the Indo-Pacific articulated in 2019 also suggests cooperation between ASEAN and forums like BIMSTEC, MGC and IORA. India has been working to infuse new energy in BIMSTEC as the regional cooperation under SAARC has been stalled due to Pakistan's tendency to bring in the Kashmir dispute. India has been conducting coordinated patrols, bilateral military exercises and the multilateral MILAN naval exercises under the Tri-Service Command at ANI.

The Indian government has planned to invest Rs 10,000 crore to develop ANI into a maritime hub including a ship repair industry. Modi government had in 2017 established Island Development Agency (IDA) for sustainable development of islands. The agency has identified 26 islands for development and 16 of those are in Andaman and Nicobar chain. Military infrastructure at ANI will be developed gradually after developing its economic potential. Militarisation of ANI will depend on China's behaviour with India. India would like to do it gradually so that the regional countries do not feel a threat from India. The pace can hasten if China becomes too assertive with India and through its military capabilities at ANI, India can exploit China's Malacca Dilemma.[19] INS Kohassa is the third naval air station at ANI commissioned in January 2019 while the current governor of ANI, Admiral D K Joshi is former naval chief which shows government's strategic outlook towards the island.[20] Given India's growing maritime security cooperation with countries like the US, France, Japan and Australia in the Indo-Pacific region, India will work with these 'like-minded' countries in future for development of ANI islands into a strategic hub.

Challenges

For India, there are some hurdles in its efforts to develop ANI as a strategic hub. ANI is environmentally sensitive area and development has to be eco-friendly and sustainable. One way to limit the impact on the environment is to have facilities built for future use and maintained with minimum manpower through the year with major deployments taking place based on the need of the hour.[21] Lack of finances is another challenge for India as the government is not able to put required amount of money to achieve desired transformation of ANI.[22] Out of the three services, Navy has the smallest budget which is not enough to fund its committed liabilities and future plans for modernisation.

NITI Aayog, the policy think tank of government of India, is working to develop the island on public-private model and may also seek participation of non-resident-Indians (NRIs) in the projects. This could potentially help the government in injecting some more money in military infrastructure on the island. Other issues pertain to bureaucratic hassles and lack of urgency in development efforts. The intra-island connectivity is also an issue and the road that links northern ANI with south is yet to be completed, this was destroyed by the 2004 tsunami.

Conclusion

Strategic importance of ANI is well recognised in India and New Delhi is making gradual efforts to transform these islands into a maritime strategic hub. India is likely to continue these efforts to make ANI a springboard for India to project maritime power in the Indo-Pacific. In this regard, India would be intensifying its maritime security cooperation with countries like the US, Japan, Australia, France and Southeast Asian countries to tap the strategic potential of ANI. At the same time, India would also build linkages between these islands and the Southeast Asian countries. Tourism and economic interdependence would be at the centre of such efforts. The pace of Indian efforts to transform ANI into a strategic hub would be determined by China's relationship with India. An assertive China could force New Delhi to inject momentum in its ANI policy. After the infamous Galwan clash between Indian and Chinese troops in 2020 and China's continued incursions in India's territory, the Quad has gained a lot of momentum and India would be looking forward to use the strategic potential of ANI. India can use its strategic geography in the IOR through the ANI to question China's continuous misbehaviour along the Line of Actual Control.

Endnotes

1   Author's interview with Commodore Somen Banerjee. (2021). *Vivekananda International Foundation*. New Delhi, July 1.

2   Mukerji, Asoke. (2021). Securing the Indian Ocean. *Indian Express*. Accessed 20th August 2021, https://indianexpress.com/article/opinion/columns/un-security-council-maritime-security-indian-ocean-7444800/

3   Chinoy, Sujan R. (2020). Time to Leverage the Strategic Potential of Andaman & Nicobar Islands. *Manohar Parrikar Institute for Defence Studies and Analyses*. Accessed 22nd August 2021, https://idsa.in/policybrief/strategic-potential-andaman-nicobar-sujanchinoy-260620

4   Author's interview with Commodore Abhay K Singh. (Retd.) (2021). *Manohar Parrikar Institute for Defence Studies and Analyses*. New Delhi. July 1.

5   Author's Email interview with Commodore R S Vasan. (Retd.). (2019). *National Maritime Foundation, Chennai Chapter*. July 8.

6   Author's interview with Abhijit Singh. (2021). *Observer Research Foundation*. New Delhi. July 12.

7   Interview with Commodore R S Vasan. (Retd.). Op. Cit.

8   Author's interview with Maj Gen P K Chakravorty. (Retd). (2021). New Delhi. July 9.

9   Interview with Commodore R S Vasan. (Retd.). Op. Cit.

10   Interview with Commodore Somen Banerjee. (2021). Op. Cit.

11   Interview with Commodore R S Vasan. (Retd.). Op. Cit.

12   Interview with Maj Gen P K Chakravorty. (Retd). Op. Cit.

13   Interview with Commodore Somen Banerjee. (2021). Op. Cit.

14   Interview with Abhijit Singh. (2021). Op. Cit.

15   Chandramohan, Balaji. (2017). The Growing Strategic Importance of the Andaman and Nicobar Islands. *Future Directions International*. Accessed 25th August 2021, https://www.futuredirections.org.au/publication/growing-strategic-importance-andaman-nicobar-islands/#_ftn3

16   Chinoy, Sujan R. (2020). Op. Cit.

17   Interview with Commodore R S Vasan. (Retd.). Op. Cit.

18   Interview with Commodore Somen Banerjee. (2021). Op. Cit.

19   Interview with Abhijit Singh. (2021). Op. Cit.

20   Interview with Commodore Somen Banerjee. (2021). Op. Cit.

21   Interview with Commodore R S Vasan. (Retd.). Op. Cit.

22   Interview with Abhijit Singh. (2021). Op. Cit.

Section IV

Internal Dynamics

Chapter 10

Rewriting the New Narrative of Jammu and Kashmir

Narender Kumar

Introduction

Disjunction between the law and state can lead to systemic decay that breeds corruption, instability, violence and erosion of institutions of governance. Jammu and Kashmir (J&K) is a victim of the disjunction that allowed the state to plunge into inexorable proxy war that not only stunted the development but also created a wide wedge between people and the government. Majoritarian view is that disjunction is caused by Article 370 and 35 A, which had given J&K a special status with regard to exercising constitutional, administrative and judicial powers. The political establishment of J&K exploited these special powers and status, leading to a lack of accountability and transparency in governance. Lack of delivery of governance was one of the main reasons for disaffection of the people with the state and the central government. Status quo suited politicians, administration, separatists and even proxies of Pakistan because there was a comfort level and an understanding between each of these actors to operate in their own domain. It was the police and central security forces who faced the brunt of proxy war that took more than 42000 lives in the last three decades. Before August 5, 2019, the semi-autonomous status of J&K allowed Pakistan to interfere and run proxy war without interruption since there was subversion in almost every institution of the state supported by political leadership that was always seen as soft towards the separatists. Article 370 was used by political leadership as a shield to prevent direct intervention by the federal agencies to bring to book radicals and separatists. Most of these institutions were favourably disposed to proxies or radicals and as a result law could never catch up with the terrorists or even the unarmed terrorists.

It was imperative to revoke Article 35A and amend Article 370 to integrate J&K fully into the Republic of India. Most important aspect to understand is that Article 370 and 35A were temporary in nature and these temporary provisions cannot be allowed to remain in vogue for indefinite period especially when these articles became a tool to give impetus to separatist movement. In fact, the accession of J&K State with India was absolute and unconditional. It was on the behest of Shaikh Abdullah that temporary provisions were inserted to give J&K a semi-autonomous status. Dr. Bhim Rao Ambedkar was unyielding on the issue of autonomy to J&K. In the conversation while framing the Indian Constitution, Dr B R Ambedkar told Shaikh Abdullah that, "to give consent to this proposal (Article 370) would be a treacherous thing against the interests of India and I, as the Law Minister of India, will never do that, I cannot betray the interests of my country".[1]

The reorganisation should not be seen as panacea against radicalisation and terrorism. This is an ongoing war and Pakistan will not let this sudden disruption derail their larger objective of bleeding India through thousand cuts, an asymmetric warfare policy being used by the Pakistan military against India since years now. It is imperative to understand that the centre of gravity will continue to remain among masses.[2] It is important to understand that if people are not with the government then, the war against terrorism will be lost. War of perception and intelligence operations can only succeed if people are with the government forces. Therefore, the government will have to be soft, empathetic and benevolent to the public who are victims of terrorism through disruptive actions of proxies of Pakistan.

Reorganisation of Jammu and Kashmir: A Step Forward

The fundamental rights of the residents of J&K were dissimilar from the residents living in the rest of India. However, these provisions became a stumbling block in development and full integration of the state into the Indian Union. Political leadership of the state and proxies of Pakistan manipulated these provisions for a separatist movement, and radicalisation of masses. As a consequence, disaffection of the people against the Indian Union rose exponentially in Kashmir Valley. It is pertinent to mention that Article 370 and 35A were temporary provisions and could not be continued for indefinite period especially when state is plagued by a separatist movement and lack of delivery of governance. People could not get benefits from the laws passed by the parliament since it was not obligatory for the state to implement these acts other than defence, external affairs, finance & communications.

It is imperative to examine what were these articles that gave dissimilar rights to the people of J&K and deprived them of large number of legislative schemes that were extended to the citizens of rest of the country. Under Article 35A, the state was allowed to make laws for citizenship (who should be the citizen or not) and ownership of property in J&K. Under Article 370, citizens from other states could not buy property in J&K.[3] The Government of India could not declare financial emergency. All laws passed by the Indian Parliament did not automatically apply to J&K while it continued to have its own flag and legislatures which were elected for six years instead of five years.[4] Such provisions gave space to the proxies of Pakistan to subvert the society and radicalised the masses since central intelligence agencies and enforcement directorate could not investigate foreign funding, links of over-ground workers with foreign proxies and misuse of funds transferred through NGOs to the religious organisations.

In a bid to remove constitutional ambiguity and anomaly, Government of India passed Reorganisation Bill, of J&K 2019, revoked Article 35A and amended Article 370. The question is how does this constitutional exercise benefit citizens and state? Most important aspect is that now all laws passed by parliament will automatically be applicable in J&K and Ladakh. The Constitution of J&K will cease to exist, and so will be the separate state flag. Non-residents can now acquire immovable property in J&K and Ladakh. State will be split into two union territories of J&K and Ladakh for ease of administration. Both of the Union Territories (UT) will have Lt Governor. However, Ladakh will not have assembly whereas, UT of J&K will continue to have assembly with 107 seats. Reservation as applicable in the rest of the country will now be authorised in both the UTs. Police and law and order will remain under the central government; however, issues related to local self-governance and land will remain with the UTs. As per the Home Minster of India, 106 central laws will now be applicable in J&K as well as the Ladakh UT with the passage of Jammu and Kashmir Reorganisation Bill, 2019 by the Parliament.[5] Some of the key benefits and legislative provisions will be applicable in J&K and Ladakh such as, prevention of corruption act, acts related to the national commission for minorities, right to education, national council for teacher education, land acquisition, national commission for *safai karamcharis*, protection of whistle-blowers, welfare of parents and senior citizens.

What the Government of India wishes to achieve through this path breaking constitutional exercise is that it will allow government to fight terrorism effectively since law & order and police will function under the Union Government. It will bring synergy among the security forces, police and intelligence agencies. Second important aspect is financial transparency and effective utilisation of central government aids and grants. Till 2016, as per Comptroller and Auditor General (CAG), J&K's debt had risen to Rs 55,358 Crores.[6] J&K has received 10 per cent of all Central grants given to states over the 2000-2016 period despite having only one per cent of the country's population. Irony is that J&K, with a population of 12.55 million according to the 2011 Census, received Rs. 91,300 per person central grant over the last sixteen years while Uttar Pradesh only received Rs. 4,300 per person over the same period.[7] In the absence of prevention of corruption act and accountability, state failed to make optimum utilisation of the financial grants and aids. The regime of corruption and misuse of public money will see an end. Third, *Gujjar*, *Bakarwal* and Schedule Cast/Schedule Tribe will get their due both in jobs and representation in legislature. Long standing demand of Valmiki (hygiene and sanitation workers) community to have reservation and citizenship will be met.

Challenges to Implement Reorganisation of J&K and Way Forward

The reorganisation of the state has altered the narrative of Pakistan and separatists. The reaction is bound to happen since this move will definitely shrink the space for separatists and Pakistan to create instability in Kashmir. Facade created by Pakistan of changing the status of J&K by India is misplaced since there are no external ramifications of this change and Line of Control (LOC) and Line of Actual Control (LAC) remains as hitherto fore. In fact status was altered by Pakistan when it illegally occupied Pakistan Occupied Jammu and Kashmir (POJK), Gilgit-Baltistan and handed over Shaksgam valley to China. Notwithstanding the above, there is need to calm down the tempers in J&K through patience, perseverance, and persistence. The canard being spread by valley based politicians, separatists and Pakistan is that newly created UTs will be colonised and reckless sale of land will take place. Government must bring in some legal framework so that people of J&K and Ladakh are assured that their interests will not be compromised.

There is a need to ensure effective governance. If the functioning of bureaucracy remains same, it is unlikely to alter the ground situation. Thus Government of India will have to ensure and put some mechanism to remove nepotism, corruption and timely execution of promised projects and schemes without dilution. The bottom line is that central government and UTs should help in removing regional imbalances and pull J&K out of economic and political instability.

Security is everyone's concern. It will be prudent to create an effective joint command structure and Jammu & Kashmir Police should be the frontline agency instead of Army or central police forces. Intra-regional engagement is must even if Ladakh is separated from J&K. The civilisational relationship should not be severed for political opportunism. It may be a good idea to create a Ministry for ensuring smooth transition of the two UTs into stable and economically empowered administrative units. This ministry under Prime Minister will be in a position to monitor and give pace to development, grievance redressal and maintenance of law and order. There is a need to identify low hanging projects that can act as confidence building measure to convey a message to the people that the reorganisation is a good for the people of J&K and Ladakh. Visible change in the governance is vital for strategic signaling.

Counterterrorism and Future Security Strategy

The security threat with the reorganisation of the state will be at an all-time high. Threat of *fidayeen* attacks within J&K and even beyond is a high probability. Jammu and rest of India can become a communal flashpoint if Pakistan is able to trigger some sensational attacks. To expect sudden end to the cross-border terrorism and proxy war will be a huge mistake. The recent events of political instability in Pakistan may create space for anti-India elements to heighten their proxy war against India. With this changed scenario, Government of India will have to fight on multiple fronts.

1. Diplomatically since Pakistan will not leave any stone unturned to raise Kashmir issue time and again at every international forum. It has already managed to push an informal close door discussion in UNSC with the help of China. In March 2022, Chinese foreign Minister Wang Yi was invited as special guest for Organisation of Islamic Cooperation (OIC) meet in Pakistan. He made some remarks on Kashmir which were rejected by India.

2. There is no letup the in infiltration bid by terrorists supported by Pakistan Army.

3. The government is now obliged to deliver governance and create jobs and kick start development as promised.

4. It is also now upon the government to showcase this move as a successful model to create pro-India wave among the POJK and Gilgit-Baltistan population.

In an uncertain and ambiguous environment, security forces should remember that sharp blows delivered against terrorists/ tactical targets have no value unless they are integrated into a broad and deep approach tackling the origins of the threat. Reorganisation of J&K is a constitutional exercise and not a panacea. It needs to be understood that firm handling of terrorism is not a muscular policy, it does not mean indiscriminate use of military, it also means use of law as a weapon and implementation of counter terrorism policies without discrimination. Recent history shows that indiscriminate military responses to terror only escalate the situation.[8] The Jammu & Kashmir state was reluctant to try separatists and terrorists arrested over the years under the charges of waging war against India. All governments past and present were guilty of not using law as deterrence against armed and unarmed terrorists. Due to cozy relationship between radicals and political leadership most of the foreign terrorists were tried for illegally crossing over to the Indian territory and illegal possession of arms whereas, they should have been tried for waging war against India. Current UT of J&K will try to rectify this anomaly. Deterrence of law is must because when terrorists are eliminated in encounters, they are considered martyrs for the cause. They should be denied an opportunity to achieve "honour in dying" by trying them for waging war against the nation.

Strategy of Patience and Perseverance through Soft Approach

Military dislodgement of terrorists is temporary but perceptional dislodgment from the community at large is what will have long term impact.The reorganisation, amendment to Article 370 and revocation of 35A should act as healing touch and not as part of majoritarian imposition of new rule. There is wisdom in investing in dislodgement of terrorists from the public perception. Soft approach does not mean appeasement but a policy of community first. Therefore, community should be used as frontline soldiers to fight battle of narrative. Community should be used to cool down the tempers of the youth and people at large. Considering the foregoing, security forces are certainly not the one that could eliminate the insurgency/ terrorism without the active participation of the people. Loss of public support is a death blow to the so called just cause of the insurgents/ terrorists. The role of the state should be to enable local population to fight terrorism by perception as well as by denial of safe haven.

There would be reversal but then security forces should come in between terrorists and public if threat is imminent. Ultimately the militancy in Punjab was defeated by active participation of the people backed by the security forces. Col. Gian Gentile, an associate professor of history at United States military academy at the West Point said, "We could lose our edge in our ability to conduct other kinds of operations"[9] if we employ hard power with a view to crush the insurgency and terrorism. If insurgencies/ terrorism could be suppressed by use of hard power, in that case Soviet Union and the United States of America (USA) could have achieved spectacular results in Vietnam, Afghanistan and in Iraq. Someone had rightly said that "Counterinsurgency and counterterrorism is known as a thinking man's war, and it has attracted some of the country's best and brightest."[10]

David Galula, French military officer and a scholar of counterinsurgency advocated that counterinsurgency is 80 per cent political and 20 per cent military. Thus, undue focus and reliance on military for conflict resolution in Kashmir is a miscalculation and unlikely to succeed unless it is backed by endeavours to win over the civil population. The perception of the government that entire population of Kashmir is dissatisfied may not be true, but if people are not treated with empathy and compassion, there is likelihood that more sections of the population may become disaffected. Counterinsurgency and counterterrorism is more holistic and it involves broader reach of power to touch the hearts and minds of the people. Radicalisation cannot be handled by muscular policy, and only way out is adoption of soft approach to deal with radical ideologies. De-radicalisation and disengagement of extremists from the toxic environment is best handled by war of ideas. It cannot be done by force; rather it requires soft approach to re-integrate the target back with the society.

Conclusion

The bottom-line of success and failure of this constitutional exercise lies in delivery of governance and redressal of grievances. Radical decisions require rationale response and it is high time for politicians and bureaucracy to leave politics out of it and ensure success of this experiment. It is true that development requires stable situation and peace and therefore, all sources that give impetus to terrorism must be neutralised. A quarter of a century ago, British Prime Minister Margaret Thatcher described publicity as the oxygen of terrorism.[11] Thus, government should not give a platform and opportunity to terror groups that give them desired mileage and publicity especially post implementation of reorganisation. No matter how many terrorists are eliminated, the cadres will continue to get replenished due to a false perception of honour to die for the cause of Jihad. The terror groups and their network is resilient and the threats they pose is too complicated to be vanquished by mere leadership and cadre decapitation.[12] Terrorists lose when cause is delegitimised by public participation. Therefore, it is important to build bridges with the people so that terror groups can be dislodged from the public perception. A new approach is required to put into practice a "dogma of muscular &soft counter terrorism" in practice. Endeavour should be to build trust with the public and deterrence against the terrorists. Let the battle of narrative be spearheaded by the people, battle of guns by the security forces and healing touch by the government.

Endnotes

1   SN Busi. (2016). *Dr. B.R. Ambedkar Framing of Indian Constitution.* New Delhi: Ava Publishers, Vol 1, Page 472.

2   John Ranie. (2018). New Priorities for International Terrorism, *International Institute for Strategic Studies*, July 21.

3   Business Standard. (2019). Explained: What are Articles 370 and 35A? Why they are important for J&K, *Business Standard*, August 05.

4   Narender Kumar. (2019). Challenges to Implement Peaceful Reorganisation of Jammu & Kashmir, *Strategic Perspective USI of India*, August 16.

5   Anand Patel. (2019). 106 central laws to apply in J&K now, *India Today*, August 7.

6   The Tribune. (2017). J&K's debt increases to Rs 55,358 cr: CAG, July 11, 2017.

7   TCA Sharad Raghavan. (2016). J&K gets 10% of Central funds with only 1% of population. *The Hindu*, July 24.

8   Simon Tisdall. (2017). The 'iron fist' response to terror attacks in Egypt never works, *The Guardian*, November 26.

9   Tara Mckelvey. (2008). The Cult of Counterinsurgency, *The American Prospect*, October 23.

10   Ibid.

11   Bruce Hoffman. (2016). The Global Terror Threat and Counterterrorism Challenges Facing the Next Administration, *CTC Sentinel*, November / December, Volume 9, Issue 11.

12   Ibid.

Chapter 11

Role of Northeast India in Act East Policy

Muzaffar Hussain

Introduction

The Post-Cold war period saw a dramatic shift in India's foreign policy. The renewed engagement with Southeast Asia through the Look East Policy was an important facet of the reorientation of India's foreign policy. Though a foreign policy strategy, Look East Policy also had a domestic resonance—with its expected association with the development of Northeast India. While India succeeded in establishing a strong economic connection with Southeast Asia, its Northeast states did not get the expected benefits. The restructuring of the Look East vision with the Act East Policy was done to address this gap and to respond to broader shifts in the strategic environment. The shift in the approach with a direct involvement of the Northeast region has been the result of a unique convergence between India's approach to neighbourhood and Indian response to the broader shifts in Asian order. This chapter attempts to situate Northeast India in the broader Look East/Act East Policy. Divided in three sections, the chapter maps the contours of Look East Policy and the attributes of Act East Policy before exploring the involvement of the Northeast India in these frameworks.

Look East and India's Foreign Policy

India's foreign policy towards Southeast Asia began with great promise. India was at the forefront of the pursuits of anti-colonialism and "pan-Asian solidarity" through initiatives like Conference on Asian relations,

Conference on Indonesia and the Bandung Conference.[1] The fear of Indian and Chinese domination pushed Southeast Asia to imagine their regionalism devoid of Indian and Chinese presence.[2] However, gap in the relations between India and the region soon emerged. India maintained a distance from Association of Southeast Asian Nations (ASEAN)— considering it a product of American (thus imperialist) design to contain Communism during the Cold War.[3] The onset of Cold war had a direct bearing on how India approached its neighbourhood—immediate and extended. The systemic environment defined by Cold-War rivalries among the blocs pushed for prioritization of security in India's approach towards its neighbours. The approach not only kept the foreign policy centred on security considerations but also prevented shaping and exploring other avenues to fundamentally transform the environment through a regional vision.[4]

The end of Cold War fundamentally transformed the structure of international system and made series of assumptions/logics informing Indian foreign policy irrelevant. Further, the collapse of Soviet Union— India's important trading partner and the experience of balance of payment crisis entailed—Indian must join the international economy and cast away the *Swadeshi* driven foreign economic policy. Indian foreign policy underwent a fundamental shift through the adoption of three key strategies: adoption of liberalization reforms, fostering relationships with United States and Israel—which were curtailed by notions of imperialism, and an outreach towards neighbourhood and extended neighbourhood— both through bilateral relations and multilateral engagements. The recasting of neighbourhood policy exhibited willingness to shape and transform the regional environment to maximize both security and economic benefits. While South Asia proved to be little difficult pursuit, Southeast Asia offered a greater promise. From economic perspective, Southeast with its success story under ASEAN offered greater prospect for India's economic growth.[5] The Look East Policy which was started by Prime Minister Narsimha Rao came in such a context and reorientation of India's foreign policy, wherein India demonstrated the willingness to join the emerging global economic order and the intention to transform terms of agreement with the neighbourhood. Through Look East Policy, India pushed for a "multi-faceted and multi-pronged" approach establishing links with individual countries in Southeast Asia and development of stronger economic and cultural relations with the ASEAN.[6] ASEAN was at the heart of India's Look East strategy. Indian overtures found positive response from ASEAN—primarily to reduce their dependence on Japan, China and the West. There was gradual progress in Indian engagement with the ASEAN. India became Sectoral Dialogue partner in 1992, Full dialogue partner in 1996, and member of Asian regional Forum in 1996.[7]

Following its inception, Look East Policy evolved with passage of time and due to other structural transformations in India's foreign policy. Prime Minister Atal Bihari Vajpayee gave a definite push to the Look East Policy as part of the broader quest to develop institutionalized engagements with Southeast Asia through multilateral framework. In this context, extensive engagement with CLMV countries—Cambodia, Laos and Vietnam was pursued and Mekong-Ganges Cooperation was established alongside series of bilateral engagements. On the ASEAN front, India moved ahead with the establishment of the Summit level –partnership. The scope of engagements with ASEAN saw an expansion with the three agreements signed on the eve of Bali Summit (2003): Framework Agreement on Comprehensive Security, Joint Declaration on Cooperation in Combating International Terrorism, and India's accession to ASEAN's Treaty of Amity and Cooperation.[8]

From the perspective of institutionalized arrangement, Indian engagement with ASEAN had a steady progress. India became the founding member of East Asia Summit (EAS)—also known as ASEAN+6, an annual security interaction—Delhi Dialogue was created and New Delhi became part of important meets like ASEAN Defence Ministers' Meeting Plus and ASEAN Maritime Security Forum.[9] These interactions and meetings succeeded in establishing a channel of interactions and allowed both economic and diplomatic exchanges. However it had limitations which were evident in three areas: it could not push economic interaction towards a regional economy through economic integration, it could not build on the security related agreements to form a joint strategic response towards the changing geo-politics and lastly, it could not properly situate and utilize the potential of Northeast region in the broader Look East strategy. The way out of these deadlocks required a re-invention of the strategy, which eventually came in form of the Act East Policy.

Reorientation of Look East to Act East Policy

At the East Asia Summit 2014, Prime Minister Narendra Modi declared the shift in India's approach towards East through the announcement of the Act East policy. With a pronounced focus on move towards greater connectivity with Southeast Asia, expansion of cultural ties and elimination of the insurgency problems in Northeast, India ushered in a paradigm shift in its Look East Policy with the new avatar—the Act East Policy.[10] The Act East policy has three key dimensions: building up on existing economic relations to push for regional connectivity and integration, formation of coherent response to strategic developments in Indo-Pacific towards preservation of rule based maritime order and the promotion of peace and development in the Northeast India. While as an economic vision, Act East Policy put in a renewed vigour in the existing initiatives under the Look East Policy, it was the strategic side which had greater significance.

Development of strategic relationship with the countries in the Indo-Pacific region (through bilateral, regional and multilateral engagements) is one of the core objectives of the Act East Policy.[11] With the defined objective as the guide, India pursued strategic partnerships with countries beyond the ASEAN region: Japan, Australia and South Korea. Though, the vision brought in actors beyond ASEAN in its ambit, ASEAN remains the focal point of the Act East strategy. As a strategic vision, the Act East Policy came simultaneously with the US declaration of the "pivot" to Asia strategy. That is, it was in sync with the broader shifts in the geo-strategic landscape of Asia and had some form of correspondence with the US response to it.

The transitions in global balance of power—with the reality of rising China—and a corresponding shifts in its behaviour forms the geo-strategic context against which Indian and American strategy is positioned. After pursuing an approach of coexistence in maritime affairs in the first decade of the millennium, China shifted to a hard-line approach in 2009. Further, China became more assertive towards disputes with India, ASEAN, Japan and other Asian countries.[12] There has been a growing convergence in Indian emphasis on role of rules based maritime order with the response of other key players in the Indo-Pacific including ASEAN. The defence framework agreement between India and US pronounced the commitment to increase the respective capability to secure "freedom of navigation across sea lanes of communication".[13] Likewise, during their meeting, PM Modi and PM Shinzo Abe asserted the commitment of the respective countries towards the "freedom of navigation and rule-based regime".[14] At the multilateral level the commitment of the Quad involving US, India, Australia and Japan towards the "prosperity and security in a free and open Indo-Pacific region" entails the development of a coherent response to the geo-strategic shifts in Indo-Pacific.[15]

Locating Northeast in the Look East/Act East Vision

Northeast India has very strategic location—sharing international borders with China, Myanmar, Bangladesh and Bhutan. The region is endowed with deposits of minerals and resources. The richness of its resources attracted traders and merchants from different parts of world like Armenia, Afghanistan, Europe and China to the region for trade.[16] Its richness also attracted East Indian Company for exploitation and control over resources. Owing to its richness in terms of resources and participation in the regional commercial activities, the region had a vibrant economic activity. The region's per capita GDP at the time of independence was 4 percent above the national average. However, the experience of partition and other geo-political developments that followed pushed the region into backwardness. Partition and other developments disrupted the traditional routes of trade, access to ports, markets and trading centres in East Bengal and Southeast Asia and thus damaged the basic structure of economic life of the region.

While recognizing the special developmental necessities of the region, Government of India attempted to address the needs through focused institutional measures. The Northeastern Council (NEC) was created in 1971 to provide financial assistance to infrastructure related projects. However, the initiative did not yield much success due to the failure to address other factors constraining the economic growth of the region. These factors include: "long-running insurgencies, disinterested governance from Delhi, endemic corruption, and tensions among the region's more than 200 ethnicities" pushed the region to the periphery of national life—both in terms of developmental growth and democratic representation.[17]

While the post-liberalization era saw the country move forward on the higher growth trajectory, growth in the region remained slow. The per capita income of the region was 20 percent lower than national average in 1990-91. The gap increased to 31 percent by 2004-25.[18] Reflecting upon the backwardness of the region, the "Transforming: The Northeast" report—also known as Shukla Commission Report (1997) identified several key shortcomings: basic needs, resources, infrastructure, governance and a "two-way deficit of understanding with the rest of the country".[19]

One of the key reasons behind the developmental deficiency of Northeast was the centrality of "security" as the framework for governance of the region. While foreign policy towards neighbours in east was dominated by security centeredness, the domestic governance of the region too was shaped by security priorities. Due to the nature of geopolitics and the state of the diplomacy with neighbours, the area became "sensitive border region".[20] The notion of sensitivity of this region from the perspective of security dominated all forms of interaction between the region and the government. In such context, the security establishment "dominated the policy in this region" and the logic of keeping the region insulated as part of security strategy dominated the policy thinking.[21]

Another important reason for failure to push development and the region and thus facilitate its integration was the presence of Delhi centric thinking and other logics/rationalities informing policies—domestic and foreign policy related with the region. One such thinking was that building of infrastructure in "border areas could provoke" neighbouring countries.[22] Thus, in a strange way keeping away from the region's development infrastructure was part of exercise of maintenance of international peace and order. Governments in Delhi were often uninterested in issues of the region.

The Look East Policy was expected to usher in developmental transformations in the North East region. The region lagged on most developmental indicators for a decade after Look East Policy. A move towards improvement of the developmental infrastructure of the region happened with the formation of the Department of Development of Northeastern Region (DoNER) in 2001, which later became the Ministry of DoNER—only Ministry of its kind with a specified territorial domain of operation. The mandate of the Ministry is implementation of the Non-Lapsable Central Pool of Resources (NLCPR) to address the gaps in infrastructure.[23] With regards to the Look East policy, formulation of a policy vision came only with the release of the Northeast Region Vision Document 2020.[24] While the document identified key areas of action—most of the policy measures conceptualized in this regard did not materialize. Even after that, the temptation to view the beginning of the "east" in Look East Policy from the place where Northeast ended continued and the region was denied an active participation in the strategy.[25]

A decisive shift in the approach both to the Northeast region and neighbourhood came with the assumption of the charge of national leadership by Narendra Modi. Among the various aspects, Modi's reformulation of Act East Policy, inclusion of Northeast in "India's outreach to South East Asian neighbourhood" was an essential component.[26] The central premise of Modi's vision was articulated by him during his stop in Tripura in December 2014. The vision as he put it involved creation of economic corridor including Northeast India, Myanmar and adjoining regions, wherein Northeast was viewed as the "gateway to Southeast Asia".

The conception of Northeast as gateway to Southeast Asia was not a policy invention out of thin air—it was rooted in the geographic and historical reality of the region. The geographical position of Northeast as the conduit between South Asia and Southeast Asia makes it a part of any policy imagination or strategy at connecting the two regions. Northeast is not just a physical space connected with Southeast Asia. The region also has strong ethnic, historical, linguistic and cultural ties with the region, which forms a unique bond between the two. While people of Meitei and Naga ethnicity also are present in Myanmar, the Tai language which is spoken in several Southeast Asian countries is also the language of Tai people living in parts of Meghalaya, Assam and Arunachal Pradesh.[27] Highlighting the significance of the region in context of the Look East policy, Wasbir Hussain (2009) has observed that: "India's Northeast can be rightly described as the beginning of Southeast Asia". The Act East Policy is not just about treating Northeast as the conduit to Southeast Asia. It is driven by the quest to overcome the hurdles of geography and policy imaginations to connect Northeast with both countries in east and rest of India.[28] New Delhi recognizes that Northeast region must be given a "special priority" so that it emerges as the "strong basis" through which it can "successfully engage with the countries across the eastern borders".[29] In this context, there has been the awareness—that successful inclusion of Northeast into the Act East Policy also requires key corrections in the approach that New Delhi had followed in its engagements with the region. A core strategy that has been employed in this regard is the improvement in the understanding of the region thus to overcome the various policy imaginations hindering Delhi's approach through strengthened communication and outreach. Regular visits to the region became the hallmark of Modi's approach towards integration of the region. Modi also gave direction to bureaucrats and union ministers to visit one North-East state on fortnightly basis—thus reducing the gap between the policy makers and people and bring Delhi right at the "doorstep of the

Northeast".[30] Also, the region's closeness to the power corridors of Delhi was ensured through the increased representation in the Union Council of Ministers through allocation of cabinet berths to representatives from the region.

Similarly, a proactive approach towards improvement of the developmental condition of the region has become a priority. There has been a steady rise in the allocation of funds to the region. The provisional expenditures by Central ministries in the region increased by 83% from Rs 24819.18 crores in 2014-15 to Rs 45,518.14 crores in 2018-19.[31] The government also instituted the NITI forum for North-East in February 2018 to deal with various developmental challenges in the region and to push sustainable economic growth in the region. Further, the deliveries of various governmental schemes have been ensured. The benefits of range of schemes like Prime Minister Awaas Yojana, Kisan Samman Nidhi, Pradhan Mantri Garib Kalyan Yojana, Ayushman Bharat Yojna, Jal Jeevan Mission have been delivered to lakhs of people in region.

An important reason why development related initiatives have not been successful in yielding result is the failure to address conflicts in the Northeast region. Conflicts in the region have contributed towards creating roadblocks to developmental initiatives. Here, the display of political will and sustained efforts to resolve issues and conflicts has been a key component of Modi's approach to the region. Several achievements were made in this regard: the signing of "Naga Peace Accord" with National Socialist Council of Nagaland (NSCN-IM), the ceasefire pact with the NSCN (K) faction, the "Bodo Peace Accord" and the "Karbi-Anglong Peace Accord".[32] Series of such initiatives are likely to built a culture of peace— and thus transform the context to make the strategy of Act East a success. There has been a substantial improvement in the conflict situation of the region. This is evident from the fact that there has been 80% reduction in insurgency related incidents between 2014 and 2021.[33] Further, due to the successful culmination of dialogues with various groups into agreements: NLFT Tripura Agreement, Bru Agreement, Bodo Peace Accord and Karbi Anglong Agreement, around 7000 militants surrendered their weapons.[34]

Along with the transformation of internal situation, Act East Policy is creating the most basic precondition for development of the region— the transport infrastructure. The conceptualization of Northeast as the "gateway to Southeast Asia" cannot become a policy reality without transportation infrastructure. Here the government has devoted attention to both international connectivity and internal connectivity. Several key projects like "Agartala-Akhaura Rail Link between India and Bangladesh, Intermodal transport linkages and inland waterways through Bangladesh, Kaladan Multimodal Transit Transport Project and the Trilateral Highway Project" are underway to establish a seamless connectivity between India and Southeast Asia.[35] While focusing on international connection with Southeast Asia, Act East strategy has put equal importance to internal connectivity within the Northeast region. Under the Bharatmala Pariyojana, and Pradhan Mantri Gram Sadak Yojana (PMGSY) road projects of thousands of kilometres have been executed to develop internal connectivity. Between 2014 and 2019, Rs 1711.9 under schemes of Ministry of DoNER and Rs 1573.56 crores have been also sanctioned for projects related with transportation infrastructure.[36]

Conclusion

The introduction of the Act East Policy is clearly one of the most important developments of India's foreign policy. Act East policy has a domestic dimension focusing on development along with a foreign policy dimension. The foreign policy side again has two aspects: economic and strategic. In context of Northeast, it is gradually emerging as the most important developmental strategy pursued by India. In case of foreign policy, it is likely to achieve both security and economic goals. The issue of security again has a direct resonance for the Northeast region. The main security problem of Northeast—the insurgency has a transnational dimension to it—with groups having financial and logistical networks across border. Here, Act East policy can facilitate a "coordinated effort by India and its neighbours" towards dismantling trans-national insurgency infrastructure.[37] The Act East unlike the Look East Policy conceptualizes the people in the region as stakeholders. This is evident from the fact that the Assam government has created a special Act East Policy Department to ensure the implementation of Act East Policy in time time-bound manner. Thus as an exercise in foreign policy with a significant domestic dimension, Act East policy is unique—in terms of its treatment of people in the Northeast region as stakeholder and participants in the wider approach towards the east.

Endnotes

1   Amitav Achary (2010), "The Idea of Asia", *Asia Policy*, 9: 32-39. Lavina
     Lee (2015) "India as a Nation of Consequence in Asia: the Potential and
     Limitations of India's 'Act East' Policy", *The Journal of East Asian Affairs*, 29
     (2): 67-104.

2   Amitav Acharya (2010).

3   ChietigiBajpaee (2017), "Deciphering India's Look East/Act East Policy",
     Contemporary Southeast Asia: A Journal of International and Strategic Affairs,
     39 (2): 348-372.

4   RubulPatgiri and Obja Borah Hazarika (2016), "Locating Northeast in
     India's Neighbourhood Policy: Transnational Solutions to the Problems of a
     Periphery", *India Quarterly*, 72(3): 235-249.

5   K.V. Kesavan (2020), "India's 'Act East' Policy and Regional Cooperation",
     Observer Research Foundation, 14 February, 2020, URL: https://
     www.orfonline.org/expert-speak/indias-act-east-policy-and-regional-
     cooperation-61375/.

6   Northeast Today(2020), "Act East Policy and Northeast: The Road Ahead",
     25, April 2020, Web, URL: https://www.northeasttoday.in/2020/04/25/act-
     east-policy-and-northeast-the-road-ahead/.

7   Zhao Hong (2007), "India and China: Rivals or Partners in Southeast Asia",
     Contemporary South East Asia, 29 (1): 121-142.

8   ChietigiBajpaee (2017).

9   Mohit Anand (2009) "India-ASEAN Relations: Analysing Regional
     Implications", IPCS Special Report, May 2009.

10   Achintya KumarDutta (2019), "Look East, Act East-II", *The Statesman*, 9
     July 2019, URL: https://www.thestatesman.com/opinion/look-east-act-
     eastii-1502775767.html.

11   MEA (2015), Ministry of External Affairs, "Question No.4062. Act East
     Policy", 23 Dec 2015,URL: http://www.mea.gov.in/lok-sabha.htm?dtl/26237/
     QUESTION_NO4062_ACT_EAST_POLICY.

12   Oba Mie (2014) "Challenges to the New ASEAN-Japan Partnership in the
     Changing Circumstances", *Japan Policy Forum*, 26 March, 2014, URL: http://
     www.japanpolicyforum.jp/archives/diplomacy/pt20140326014352.html.

13   Indian Express (2015*)*, "India's Act East Policy balancing China in the Region:
     Think Tank", *Indian Express,* 24 July, 2015,URL: https://indianexpress.com/

article/india/india-others/indias-act-east-policy-balancing-china-in-the-region-thinktank/.

14   Tang Ming Hui and Nazia Hussain (2017), "Japan and India: Concerted Efforts at Regional Diplomacy", *The Diplomat*, 10, April 2017, https://thediplomat.com/2017/04/japan-and-india-concerted-efforts-at-regional-diplomacy/.

15   Maha Siddiqui (2017), "India Looks to Balance Regional Equations with China After Quad Talks", *CNN-NEWS 18*, 6 Dec. 2017, http://www.news18.com/news/india/india-looks-to-balance-regional-equations-with-china-after-quad-talks-1596967.html.

16   RubulPatgiri and Obja Borah Hazarika (2016).

17   WasbirHussain (2009), "India's Norheast: The Super-highway to Southeast Asia?", *IPCS Issue Brief*, June 2009, No. 104.Edmund Downie (2014), "Narendra Modi's Northeast India Outreach", The Diplomat, 14 December, 2024, URL: https://thediplomat.com/2014/12/narendra-modis-northeast-india-outreach/.

18   Wasbir Hussain (2009).

19   Jayanta Madhab (2020), "The Story of North East Vision 2020", *Dialogue*, 10 (3), URL: http://www.asthabharati.org/Dia_Jan%2009/madh.html.

20   Sanjib Baruah (2005), *Durable disorder: Understanding the politics of northeast India*. New Delhi: Oxford University Press.

21   Sreeradha Datta (2021), *Act East Policy and Northeast India,* Delhi: Vitasta.

22   Himanta Biswa Sarma (2021), "India's North-east, from the periphery to the core", *The Hindu*, 15 August, 2021.

23   Raile RockyZiipao (2020), "Deepening Critical Infrastructures in Northeast India: People's Perspective and Policy Implications", *Strategic Analysis*, 44(3): 208-233.

24   Gorky Chakraborty (2012), "Northeast Vision 2020: A Reality Check", Occasional Paper No. 33, Institute of Development Studies Kolkatta, URL: http://idsk.edu.in/wp-content/uploads/2015/07/OP-33.pdf.

25   Mukesh Rawat (2014), "India Should Look East, to Northeast India", *The Diplomat*, 19 November, 2014, URL: https://thediplomat.com/2014/11/india-should-look-east-to-northeast-india/.

26   Sreeradha Datta (2021).

27 StanzinLhaskyab (2022), "How AFSPA Undermines India's 'Act East' Policy", *The Diplomat,* 4 January, 2022, URL: https://thediplomat.com/2022/01/how-afspa-undermines-indias-act-east-policy/.

28 Achintya Kumar Dutta (2019), "Look East, Act East-II", *The Statesman,* 9 July 2019, URL: https://www.thestatesman.com/opinion/look-east-act-eastii-1502775767.html.

29 PIB (2021), Press Information Bureau, "Union Minister Dr. Jitendra delivers keynote address on "Act East Policy" webinar organized by ICRIER", Press Release, 20 March, 2021, URL: https://pib.gov.in/PressReleaseIframePage.aspx?PRID=1706296.

30 Raju Bista (2021), "Decisive governance: A new paradigm that is transforming the northeast", *India Today,* 26 September, 2021, URL: https://www.indiatoday.in/opinion-columns/story/decisive-governance-a-new-paradigm-that-is-transforming-northeast-1857395-2021-09-26.

31 PIB (2019), Press Information Bureau, "Northeastern Region Vision 2020", Press Release, 25 July, 2019, URL: https://pib.gov.in/Pressreleaseshare.aspx?PRID=1580240.

32 Raju Bista (2021).

33 Himanta Biswa Sarma (2021).

34 Subimal Bhattacharjee (2022), "Towards a peaceful, stable Northeast", *The Indian Express,* 20 April, 2022, URL: https://indianexpress.com/article/opinion/columns/towards-a-peaceful-stable-northeast-7877246/.

35 PIB (2021).

36 PIB (2019).

37 RubulPatgiri and Obja Borah Hazarika (2016).

Appendices

Appendix I
(Refers to Page 36)

Sardar Patel's Letter to Prime Minister Jawaharlal Nehru

New Delhi

7 November 1950

My Dear Jawaharlal,

Ever since my return from Ahmedabad and after the cabinet meeting the same day which I had to attend at practically 15 minutes' notice and for which I regret I was not able to read all the papers, I have been anxiously thinking over the problem of Tibet and I thought I should share with you what is passing through my mind.

I have carefully gone through the correspondence between the External Affairs Ministry and our Ambassador in Peking and through him the Chinese Government. I have tried to peruse this correspondence as favourably to our Ambassador and the Chinese Government as possible, but I regret to say that neither of them comes out well as a result of this study. The Chinese Government has tried to delude us by professions of peaceful intention. My own feeling is that at a crucial period they manage to instil into our Ambassador a false sense of confidence in their so-called desire to settle the Tibetan problem by peaceful means. There can be no doubt that during the period covered by this correspondence the Chinese must have been concentrating for an onslaught on Tibet. The final action of the Chinese, in my judgment, is little short of perfidy. The tragedy of it is that the Tibetans put faith in us; they choose to be guided by us, and we have been unable to get them out of the meshes of Chinese diplomacy or Chinese malevolence. From the latest position, it appears that we shall not be able to rescue the Dalai Lama. Our Ambassador has been at great pains to find an explanation or justification for Chinese policy and actions. As the External Affairs Ministry remarked in one of their telegrams, there was a lack of firmness and unnecessary apology in one or two representations that he made to the Chinese Government on our behalf. It is impossible to imagine any sensible person believing in the so-called threat to China from Anglo-American machinations in Tibet. Therefore, if the Chinese put faith in this, they must have distrusted us so completely as to have taken us as tools or stooges of Anglo-American diplomacy or strategy. This feeling, if genuinely entertained by the Chinese in spite of your direct approaches to them, indicates that even though we regard ourselves as friends of China, the Chinese do not regard us as their friends. With the Communist mentality of "whoever is not with them being against them," this is a significant pointer, of which we have to take due note. During the last several months, outside the Russian camp, we have practically been alone in championing the cause of Chinese entry into UN and in securing from the Americans assurances on the question of Formosa. We have done everything we could to assuage Chinese feelings, to allay its apprehensions and to defend its legitimate claims in our discussions and correspondence with America and Britain and in the UN. In spite of this, China is not convinced about our disinterestedness; it continues to regard us with suspicion and the whole psychology is one, at least outwardly, of scepticism perhaps mixed with a little hostility. I doubt if we can go any further that we have done already to convince China of our good intentions, friendliness and goodwill. In Peking, we have an Ambassador who is eminently suitable for putting across the friendly point of view. Even he seems to have failed to convert the Chinese. Their last telegram to us is an act of gross discourtesy not only in the summary way it disposes of our protest against the entry of Chinese forces into Tibet but also in the wild insinuation that our attitude is determined by foreign influences. It looks as though it is not a friend speaking in that language but a potential enemy.

In the background of this, we have to consider what new situation now faces us as a result of the disappearance of Tibet, as we knew it, and the expansion of China almost up to our gates. Throughout history we have seldom been worried about our north-east frontier. The Himalayas have been regarded as an impenetrable barrier against any threat from the north. We had friendly Tibet which gave us no trouble. The Chinese were divided. They had their own domestic problems and never bothered us about frontiers. In 1914, we entered into a convention with Tibet which was not endorsed by the Chinese. We seem to have regarded Tibetan autonomy as extending to independent treaty relationship. Presumably, all that we required was Chinese counter-signature. The Chinese interpretation of suzerainty seems to be different. We can, therefore, safely assume that very soon they will disown all the stipulations which Tibet has entered into with us in the past. That throws into the melting pot all frontier and commercial settlements with Tibet on which we have been functioning and acting during the last half a century. China is no longer divided. It is united and strong. All along the Himalayas in the north and north-east, we have on our side of the frontier a population ethnologically and culturally not different from Tibetans and Mongoloids. The undefined state of the frontier and the existence on our side of a population with its affinities to the Tibetans or Chinese have all the elements of the potential trouble between China and ourselves. Recent and bitter history also tells us that communism is no shield against imperialism and that the communist are as good or as bad imperialist as any other. Chinese ambitions in this respect not only covered the Himalayan slopes on our side but also include the important part of Assam. They have their ambitions in Burma also. Burma has the added difficulty that it has no McMohan line round which to build up even the semblance of an agreement. Chinese irredentism and communist imperialism are different from the expansionism or imperialism of the western powers. The former has a cloak of ideology which makes it ten times more dangerous. In the guise of ideological expansion lie concealed racial, national or historical claims. The danger from the north and north-east, therefore, becomes both communist and imperialist. While our western and non-western threat to security is still as prominent as before, a new threat has developed from the north and north-east. Thus, for the first time, after centuries, India's defence has to concentrate itself on two fronts simultaneously. Our defence measures have so far been based on the calculations of superiority over Pakistan. In our calculations we shall now have to reckon with communist China in the north and in the north-east, a communist China which has definite ambitions and aims and which does not, in any way, seem friendly disposed towards us.

Let us also consider the political conditions on this potentially troublesome frontier. Our northern and north-eastern approaches consist of Nepal, Bhutan, Sikkim, the Darjeeling (area) and tribal areas in Assam. From the point of view of communication, there are weak spots. Continuous defensive lines do not exist. There is almost an unlimited scope for infiltration. Police protection is limited to a very small number of passes. There, too, our outposts do not seem to be fully manned. The contact of these areas with us is by no means close and intimate. The people inhabiting these portions have no established loyalty or devotion to India even the Darjeeling and Kalimpong areas are not free from pro-Mongoloid prejudices. During the last three years we have not been able to make any appreciable approaches to the Nagas and other hill tribes in Assam. European missionaries and other visitors had been in touch with them, but their influence was in no way friendly to India/Indians. In Sikkim, there was political ferment some time ago. It is quite possible that discontent is smouldering there. Bhutan is comparatively quiet, but its affinity with Tibetans would be a handicap. Nepal has a weak oligarchic regime based almost entirely on force; it is in conflict with a turbulent element of the population as well as with enlightened ideas of modern age. In these circumstances, to make people alive to the new danger or to make them defensively strong is a very difficult task indeed and that difficulty can be got over only by enlightened firmness, strength and a clear line of policy. I am sure the Chinese and their source of inspiration, Soviet Union would not miss any opportunity of exploiting these weak spots, partly in support of their ideology and partly in support of their ambitions. In my judgment, the situation is one which we cannot afford either to be complacent or to be vacillating. We must have a clear idea of what we wish to achieve and also of the methods by which we should achieve it. Any faltering or lack of decisiveness in formulating our objectives or in pursuing our policies to attain those objectives is bound to weaken us and increase the threats which are so evident.

Side by side with these external dangers, we shall now have to face serious internal problems as well. I have already asked (HVR) Iyengar to send to the EA Ministry a copy of the Intelligence Bureau's appreciation of these matters. Hitherto, the Communist party of India has found some difficulty in contacting communists abroad, or in getting supplies of arms, literature, etc., from them. They had to contend with the difficult Burmese and Pakistan frontiers on the east with the long seaboard. They shall now have a comparatively easy means of access to Chinese communists and through them to other foreign communists. Infiltration of spies, fifth columnists and communists would now be easier. Instead of having to deal with isolated communist pockets and Telengana and Warangal we may have to deal with communist threats to our security along our northern and north-eastern frontiers, where, for supplies of arms and ammunition, they can safely depend on communist arsenals in China. The whole situation thus raises a number of problems on which we must come to early decision so that we can, as I said earlier, formulate the objectives of our policy and decide the method by which those objectives are to be attained. It is also clear that the action will have to be fairly comprehensive, involving not only our defence strategy and state of preparations but also problem of internal security to deal with which we have not a moment to lose. We shall also have to deal with administrative and political problems in the weak spots along the frontier to which I have already referred.

It is of course, impossible to be exhaustive in setting out all these problems. I am, however, giving below some of the problems which in my opinion, require early solution and round which we have to build our administrative or military policies and measures to implement them.

(a) A military and intelligence appreciation of the Chinese threat to India both on the frontier and to internal security.

(b) An examination of military position and such redisposition of our forces as might be necessary, particularly with the idea of guarding important routes or areas which are likely to be the subject of dispute.

(c) An appraisement of strength of our forces and, if necessary, reconsideration of our retrenchment plans to the Army in the light of the new threat. A long-term consideration of our defence needs. My own feeling is that, unless we assure our supplies of arms, ammunition and armour, we should be making a defence position perpetually weak and we would not be able to stand up to the double threat of difficulties both from the west and north and north-east.

(d) The question of Chinese entry into UN. In view of rebuff which China has given us and the method which it has followed in dealing with Tibet, I am doubtful whether we can advocate its claims any longer. There would probably be a threat in the UN virtually to outlaw China in view of its active participation in the Korean War. We must determine our attitude on this question also.

(e) The political and administrative steps which we should take to strengthen our northern and north-eastern frontier. This would include whole of border, i.e., Nepal, Bhutan, Sikkim, Darjeeling and tribal territory of Assam.

(f) Measures of internal security in the border areas as well as the states flanking those areas such as U.P., Bihar, Bengal and Assam.

(g) Improvement of our communication, road, rail, air and wireless, in these areas and with the frontier outposts.

(h) The future of our mission at Lhasa and the trading post of Gyangtse and Yatung and the forces which we have in operation in Tibet to guard the trade routes.

(i) The policies in regards to McMohan line.

These are some of the questions which occur to my mind. It is possible that a consideration of these matters may lead us into wider question of our relationship with China, Russia, America, Britain and Burma. This, however would be of a general nature, though some might be basically very important, i.e., we might have to consider whether we should not enter into closer association with Burma in order to strengthen the latter in its dealings with China. I do not rule out the possibility that, before applying pressure on us, China might apply pressure on Burma. With Burma, the frontier is entirely undefined and the Chinese territorial claims are more substantial. In its present position, Burma might offer an easier problem to China, and, therefore, might claim its first attention.

I suggest that we meet early to have a general discussion on these problems and decide on such steps as we might think to be immediately necessary and direct, quick examination of other problems with a view to taking early measure to deal with them.

Yours,

Vallabhbhai Patel

Prime Minister's Keynote Address at Shangri La Dialogue
(June 01, 2018)

June 01, 2018

Prime Minister Lee Hsien Loong,

Thank you for your friendship, your leadership of India-Singapore partnership and a better future for the region. Defence Ministers, Mr. John Chipman, Dignitaries and Excellencies,

Namaskar and a very good evening to all of you!

I am pleased to return to a region, known to India since ancient times as सुवर्णभूमि, (the land of gold). I am also happy to be here in a special year, in a land-mark year of India's relationship with ASEAN. In January, we had the unique honour of hosting ten ASEAN leaders on our Republic Day. The ASEAN-India Summit was a testimony of our commitment to ASEAN, and to our Act East policy.

For thousands of years, Indians have turned to the East. Not just to see the Sun rise, but also to pray for its light to spread over the entire world. The human-kind now looks to the Rising East, with the hope to see the promise that this 21st century beholds for the whole world, because the destiny of the world will be deeply influenced by the course of developments in the Indo-Pacific region.

Because, this new age of promise is also caught in shifting plates of global politics and the fault lines of history. I am here to say that the future we seek does not have to be as elusive as Shangri La; that we can shape this region in our collective hopes and aspirations. Nowhere is it more apt to pursue this than in Singapore. This great nation shows us that when the oceans are open, the seas are secure, countries are connected, the rule of law prevails and the region is stable, nations, small and large; prosper as sovereign countries, free and fearless in their choices.

Singapore also shows that when nations stand on the side of principles, not behind one power or the other, they earn the respect of the world and a voice in international affairs. And, when they embrace diversity at home, they seek an inclusive world outside.

For India, though, Singapore means more. It's the spirit that unites a lion nation and a lion city. Singapore is our springboard to ASEAN. It has been, for centuries, a gateway for India to the East. For over two thousand years, the winds of monsoons, the currents of seas and the force of human aspirations have built timeless links between India and this region. It was cast in peace and friendship, religion and culture, art and commerce, language and literature. These human links have lasted, even as the tides of politics and trade saw their ebb and flow.

Over the past three decades, we have re-claimed that heritage to restore our role and relationships in the region. For India, no region now receives as much attention as this and for good reasons.

Oceans had an important place in Indian thinking since pre-Vedic times. Thousands of years ago, the Indus Valley Civilisation as well as Indian peninsula had maritime trade. Oceans and Varuna – the Lord of all Waters – find a prominent place in the world's oldest books- the Vedas. In ancient Puranas, written thousands of years ago, the geographical definition of India is with reference to the seas: उत्तरों यत समुद्रस्य meaning, the land which lies to the north of the seas.

Lothal, in my home state Gujarat, was among the world's oldest ports. Even today there are remains of a dock. No wonder Gujaratis are enterprising and travel widely even today! The Indian Ocean has shaped much of India's history. It now holds the key to our future. The ocean carries 90% of India's trade and our energy sources. It is also the life line of global commerce. The Indian Ocean connects regions of diverse cultures and different levels of peace and prosperity. It also now bears ships of major powers. Both raise concerns of stability and contest.

To the East, the Malacca Strait and South China Sea connect India to the Pacific and to most of our major partners - ASEAN, Japan, Republic of Korea, China and the Americas.Our trade in the region is growing rapidly. And, a significant part of our overseas investments flow in this direction. ASEAN alone accounts for over 20%.

Our interests in the region are vast, and our engagement is deep. In the Indian Ocean region, our relationships are becoming stronger. We are also helping build economic capabilities and improve maritime security for our friends and partners. We promote collective security through forums like Indian Ocean Naval Symposium.

We are advancing a comprehensive agenda of regional co-operation through Indian Ocean Rim Association. And, we also work with partners beyond the Indian Ocean Region to ensure that the global transit routes remain peaceful and free for all.

Three years ago, in Mauritius, I described our vision in one word – Sagar, which means ocean in Hindi. And, Sagar stands for Security and Growth for All in the Region and, that is the creed we follow to our East now even more vigorously through our Act East Policy by seeking to join India, especially her East and North-East, with our land and maritime partners to the east.

South-east Asia is our neighbour by land and sea. With each Southeast Asian country, we have growing political, economic and defence ties. With ASEAN, from dialogue partners, we have become strategic partners over the course of 25 years. We pursue our relations through annual summits and 30 dialogue mechanisms, but even more through a shared vision for the region, and the comfort and familiarity of our old links.

We are active participants in ASEAN-led institutions like East Asia Summit, A.D.M.M. Plus and A.R.F. We are part of BIMSTEC and Mekong-Ganga Economic Corridor - a bridge between South and Southeast Asia.

Our ties with Japan – from economic to strategic – have been completely transformed. It is a partnership of great substance and purpose that is a corner-stone of India's Act East Policy. There is a strong momentum in our cooperation with Republic of Korea. And, there is a fresh energy in our partnerships with Australia, as also New Zealand.

With several of our partners, we meet in formats of three or more. More than three years ago, I landed at dawn in Fiji to start a successful new phase of engagement with Pacific Island Nations. The meetings of the Forum for India-Pacific Islands Cooperation, or FIPIC, have bridged the distance of geography through shared interests and action.

Beyond East and Southeast Asia, our partnerships are strong and growing. It is a measure of our strategic autonomy that India's Strategic Partnership, with Russia, has matured to be special and privileged.

Ten days ago in an informal summit at Sochi, President Putin and I shared our views on the need for a strong multi-polar world order for dealing with the challenges of our times. At the same time, India's global strategic partnership with the United States has overcome the hesitations of history and continues to deepen across the extraordinary breadth of our relationship. It has assumed new significance in the changing world. And, an important pillar of this partnership is our shared vision of an open, stable, secure and prosperous Indo-Pacific Region. No other relationship of India has as many layers as our relations with China. We are the world's two most populous countries and among the fastest growing major economies. Our cooperation is expanding. Trade is growing. And, we have displayed maturity and wisdom in managing issues and ensuring a peaceful border.

In April, a two-day informal Summit with President Xi helped us cement our understanding that strong and stable relations between our two nations are an important factor for global peace and progress. I firmly believe that, Asia and the world will have a better future when India and China work together in trust and confidence, sensitive to each other's interests.

India has a growing partnership with Africa, propelled through mechanisms such as India-Africa Forum Summits. At its core are cooperation based on Africa's requirements, and a history of warmth and mutual respect.

Friends,

Coming back to our region, India's growing engagement is accompanied by deeper economic and defence cooperation. We have more trade agreements in this part of the world than in any other. We have Comprehensive Economic Partnership Agreements with Singapore, Japan and South Korea.

We have Free Trade Agreements with ASEAN and Thailand. And, we are now actively participating in concluding the Regional Comprehensive Economic Partnership Agreement. I have just paid my first visit to Indonesia, India's neighbour 90 nautical miles close, and not 90 nautical miles apart.

My friend President Widodo and I upgraded India-Indonesia relations to a Comprehensive Strategic Partnership. Among other shared interests, we have a common vision for maritime cooperation in the Indo-Pacific. On way from Indonesia, I stopped over briefly in Malaysia to meet one of ASEAN's most senior leaders, Prime Minister Mahathir.

Friends,

India Armed Forces, especially our Navy, are building partnerships in the Indo-Pacific region for peace and security, as well as humanitarian assistance and disaster relief. They train, exercise and conduct goodwill missions across the region. For example, with Singapore, we have the longest un-interrupted naval exercise, which is in its twenty fifth year now. We will start a new tri-lateral exercise with Singapore soon and we hope to extend it to other ASEAN countries. We work with partners like Vietnam to build mutual capabilities. India conducts Malabar Exercise with the United States and Japan. A number of regional partners join in India's Exercise Milan in the Indian Ocean, and participate in RIMPAC in the Pacific.

We are active in the Regional Cooperation Agreement on Combating Piracy and Armed Robbery against Ships in Asia – in this very city. Distinguished members of the audience, Back home, our principal mission is transforming India to a New India by 2022, when Independent India will be 75 years young.

We will sustain growth of 7.5 to 8% per year. As our economy grows, our global and regional integration will increase. A nation of over 800 million youth knows that their future will be secured not just by the scale of India's economy, but also by the depth of global engagement. More than anywhere else, our ties will deepen and our presence will grow in the region. But, the future we seek to build needs stable bedrock of peace. And, this is far from certain.

There are shifts in global power, change in the character of global economy and daily disruption in technology. The foundations of the global order appear shaken. And, the future looks less certain. For all our progress, we live on the edge of uncertainty, of unsettled questions and unresolved disputes; contests and claims; and clashing visions and competing models. We see growing mutual insecurity and rising military expenditure; internal dislocations turning into external tensions; and new fault lines in trade and competition in the global commons. Above all, we see assertion of power over re-course to international norms. In the midst of all this, there are challenges that touch us all, including the un-ending threat of terrorism and extremism. This is a world of inter-dependent fortunes and failures. And, no nation can shape and secure it on its own.

It is a world that summons us to rise above divisions and competition to work together. Is that possible?

Yes. It is possible. I see ASEAN as an example and inspiration. ASEAN represents the greatest level of diversity of culture, religion, language, governance and prosperity of any grouping in the world.

It was born when Southeast Asia was a frontline of global competition, a theatre of a brutal war and a region of uncertain nations. Yet, today, ASEAN has united ten countries behind a common purpose. ASEAN unity is essential for a stable future for this region.

And, each of us must support it, not weaken it. I have attended four East Asia Summits. I am convinced that ASEAN can integrate the broader region. In many ways, ASEAN is already leading the process. In doing so, it has laid the foundation of the Indo-Pacific Region. The East Asia Summit and the Regional Comprehensive Economic Partnership – two important initiatives of ASEAN – embrace this geography.

Friends,

The Indo-Pacific is a natural region. It is also home to a vast array of global opportunities and challenges. I am increasingly convinced with each passing day that the destinies of those of us who live in the region are linked. Today, we are being called to rise above divisions and competition to work together.

The ten countries of South East Asia connect the two great oceans in both the geographical and civilisational sense. Inclusiveness, openness and ASEAN centrality and unity, therefore, lie at the heart of the new Indo-Pacific. India does not see the Indo-Pacific Region as a strategy or as a club of limited members.

Nor as a grouping that seeks to dominate. And by no means do we consider it as directed against any country. A geographical definition, as such, cannot be. India's vision for the Indo-Pacific Region is, therefore, a positive one. And, it has many elements.

One, it stands for a free, open, inclusive region, which embraces us all in a common pursuit of progress and prosperity. It includes all nations in this geography as also others beyond who have a stake in it.

Two, Southeast Asia is at its centre. And, ASEAN has been and will be central to its future. That is the vision that will always guide India, as we seek to cooperate for architecture for peace and security in this region.

Three, we believe that our common prosperity and security require us to evolve, through dialogue, a common rules-based order for the region. And, it must equally apply to all individually as well as to the global commons. Such an order must believe in sovereignty and territorial integrity, as well as equality of all nations, irrespective of size and strength. These rules and norms should be based on the consent of all, not on the power of the few. This must be based on faith in dialogue, and not dependence on force. It also means that when nations make international commitments, they must uphold them. This is the foundation of India's faith in multilateralism and regionalism; and, of our principled commitment to rule of law.

Four, we should all have equal access as a right under international law to the use of common spaces on sea and in the air that would require freedom of navigation, unimpeded commerce and peaceful settlement of disputes in accordance with international law. When we all agree to live by that code, our sea lanes will be pathways to prosperity and corridors of peace. We will also be able to come together to prevent maritime crimes, preserve marine ecology, protect against disasters and prosper from blue economy.

Five, this region, and all of us, have benefitted from globalisation. Indian food is among the best examples of these benefits! But, there is growing protectionism – in goods and in services. Solutions cannot be found behind walls of protection, but in embracing change. What we seek is a level playing field for all. India stands for open and stable international trade regime. We will also support rule-based, open, balanced and stable trade environment in the Indo-Pacific Region, which lifts up all nations on the tide of trade and investment. That is what we expect from Regional Comprehensive Economic Partnership. RCEP must be comprehensive, as the name suggests, and the principles declared. It must have a balance among trade, investment and services.

Six, connectivity is vital. It does more than enhance trade and prosperity. It unites a region. India has been at the crossroads for centuries. We understand the benefits of connectivity. There are many connectivity initiatives in the region. If these have to succeed, we must not only build infrastructure, we must also build bridges of trust. And for that, these initiatives must be based on respect for sovereignty and territorial integrity, consultation, good governance, transparency, viability and sustainability. They must empower nations, not place them under impossible debt burden. They must promote trade, not strategic competition. On these principles, we are prepared to work with everyone. India is doing its part, by itself and in partnership with others like Japan – in South Asia and Southeast Asia, in the Indian Ocean, Africa, West Asia and beyond. And, we are important stake-holders in New Development Bank and the Asian Infrastructure Investment Bank.

Finally, all of this is possible, if we do not return to the age of great power rivalries I have said this before: Asia of rivalry will hold us all back. Asia of cooperation will shape this century. So, each nation must ask itself: Are its choices building a more united world, or forcing new divisions? It is a responsibility that both existing and rising powers have. Competition is normal. But, contests must not turn into conflict; differences must not be allowed to become disputes. Distinguished members of the audience, It is normal to have partnerships on the basis of shared values and interests. India, too, has many in the region and beyond.

We will work with them, individually or in formats of three or more, for a stable and peaceful region. But, our friendships are not alliances of containment. We choose the side of principles and values, of peace and progress, not one side of a divide or the other. Our relationships across the world speak for our position.

And, when we can work together, we will be able to meet the real challenges of our times. We will be able to protect our planet. We will be able to ensure non-proliferation. We will be able to secure our people from terrorism and cyber threats.

In conclusion, let me say this again: India's own engagement in the Indo-Pacific Region – from the shores of Africa to that of the Americas - will be inclusive. We are inheritors of Vedanta philosophy that believes in essential oneness of all, and celebrates unity in diversity एकम सत्यम, विप्राः बहुदावदंति (Truth is one; the learned speak of it in many ways). That is the foundation of our civilisational ethos – of pluralism, co-existence, openness and dialogue. The ideals of democracy that define us as a nation also shape the way we engage the world.

So, it translates into five S in Hindi: सम्मान (respect); सम्वाद (dialogue); सह्योग (cooperation), शांति (peace), and समृद्धि (prosperity). It's easy to learn these words! So, we will engage with the world in peace, with respect, through dialogue and absolute commitment to international law.

We will promote a democratic and rules-based international order, in which all nations, small and large, thrive as equal and sovereign. We will work with others to keep our seas, space and airways free and open; our nations secure from terrorism; and our cyber space free from disruption and conflict. We will keep our economy open and our engagement transparent. We will share our resources, markets and prosperity with our friends and partners. We will seek a sustainable future for our planet, as through the new International Solar Alliance together with France and other partners.

This is how we wish ourselves and our partners to proceed in this vast region and beyond. The ancient wisdom of the region is our common heritage. Lord Buddha's message of peace and compassion has connected us all. Together, we have contributed much to human civilisation. And, we have been through the devastation of war and the hope of peace. We have seen the limits of power. And, we have seen the fruits of cooperation.

This world is at a crossroad. There are temptations of the worst lessons of history. But, there is also a path of wisdom. It summons us to a higher purpose: to rise above a narrow view of our interests and recognise that each of us can serve our interests better when we work together as equals in the larger good of all nations. I am here to urge all to take that path.

Thank you.

Thank you very much.

Bibliography

Akbar, M. J. (2018). *Kashmir: Behind the Vale*. Roli Books.

Bajpai, Kanti. (2021). *India Versus China: Why they are Not Friends*. Juggernaut.

Behera, Laxman Kumar. (2020). *India's Defence Economy Planning, Budgeting, Industry and Procurement*. Taylor & Francis.

Brewster, David. (2014). *India's Ocean: The Story of India's Bid for Regional Leadership*. Taylor & Francis.

Brewster, David. (2018). *India and China at Sea Competition for Naval Dominance in the Indian Ocean*. OUP India.

Chakravorty, P. K. (2019). *Assessment of Chinese Military Modernisation and Its Implications for India*. Vivekananda International Foundation.

Chandra, Satish & Baladas Ghoshal. (2018). *The Indo-Pacific Axis Peace and Prosperity Or Conflict?*. Taylor & Francis.

Das, Gurudas & C. Joshua Thomas. (2016). *Look East to Act East Policy Implications for India's Northeast*. Taylor & Francis.

Dogra, Rajiv. (2020). *India's World How Prime Ministers Shaped Foreign Policy*. Rupa.

De, Prabir. (2020). *Act East to Act Indo-Pacific India's Expanding Neighbourhood*. KW Publishers Pvt Limited.

Ganguly, Anirban. et. al. (2016). *The Modi Doctrine New Paradigms in India's Foreign Policy*. Wisdom Tree Publishers.

Gokhale, Vijay. (2021). *The Long Game: How the Chinese Negotiate with India*. Penguin.

Gupta, Arvind. (2018). *How India Manages Its National Security*. Penguin Random House India Private Limited.

Haokip, Thongkholal. (2015).

Jagmohan. (2017). *My Frozen Turbulence in Kashmir*. Allied Publishers Private Limited.

Jaishankar, Dhruva. (2019). *Acting East India in the Indo-Pacific*. Brookings India.

Jaishankrar, S. (2020). *The India Way Strategies for an Uncertain World*. Harper Collins India.

Lele, Ajay. (2021). *Quantum Technologies and Military Strategy*. Springer.

Lintner, Bertil. (2019). *The Costliest Pearl China's Struggle for India's Ocean*. Hurst.

Mallik, Amitav. (2016). *Role of Technology in International Affairs*. Pentagon Press.

Mohan, C. Raja (2012). *Samudra Manthan Sino-Indian Rivalry in the Indo-Pacific*. Brookings Institution Press.

Mukherjee, Anit. (2019). *The Absent Dialogue Politicians, Bureaucrats, and the Military in India*. Oxford University Press.

Muni, S. D. & Rahul Mishra. (2019). *India's Eastward Engagement From Antiquity to Act East Policy*. Sage Publications.

Panag, H. S. (2020). *The Indian Army Reminiscences, Reforms & Romance*. Westland Publications Private Limited.

Pande, Aparna. (2017). *From Chanakya to Modi Evolution of India's Foreign Policy*. HarperCollins Publishers India.

Pant, Harsh. V. (2016). *Handbook of Indian Defence Policy Themes, Structures and Doctrines*. Taylor & Francis.

Pant, Harsh V. (2019). *Indian Foreign Policy: The Modi Era*. Har-Anand Publications Pvt Limited.

Kaushiva, Pradeep & Abhijit Singh. (2014). *Geopolitics of the Indo-Pacific*. KW Publishers.

Kumar, Pramod Roy. & N. M. Aspi Cawasji. (2017). *Strategic Vision-2030: Security and Development of Andaman & Nicobar Islands*. Vij Books India Pvt Limited.

Sarma, Atul & Saswati Choudhary. (2017). *Mainstreaming the Northeast in India's Look and Act East Policy*. Springer Singapore.

Singh, M Amarjeet. (2019). *Northeast India and India's Act East Policy Identifying the Priorities*. Taylor & Francis.

Singh, Sinderpal. (2017). *Modi And The World: (Re) Constructing Indian Foreign Policy*. World Scientific Publishing Company.

Wadhwa, Anil & Arvind Gupta (2020). *India's Foreign Policy Surviving in a Turbulent World*. Sage Publications.

Index

About the Editor

Dr. Nivedita Das Kundu, (Ph.D) is a distinguished academic with extensive experience in university teaching and think tank research, specializing in International Relations. She is affiliated with the York University in Toronto and Alatoo-International University, Bishkek, where she holds Associate Professors position in International Relations. She is presently teaching Bachelor's and Master's students and supervising Ph.D students at a State University in Tashkent under Ministry of Higher Education, Science and Innovation of Republic of Uzbekistan, as an Associate Professor of International Relations.

Dr. Nivedita's educational background includes a Master's and doctoral studies from Jawaharlal Nehru University, New Delhi, and the University of Helsinki, Finland. She further pursued post-doctoral studies at the Woodrow Wilson Centre for Scholars in Washington DC. Throughout her career, she has contributed to academia and research by teaching at renowned institutions across the globe, including universities in Canada, Germany, Finland, India, Kyrgyzstan, Kazakhstan, Russia, China and Azerbaijan. Her expertise has been sought after by prestigious government think tanks such as the Institute for Defence Studies and Analyses, Indian

170

Council for World Affairs, Indian Council for Social Science Research, United Services Institution of India, and the Centre for Strategic Studies under the President of Azerbaijan.

Dr. Nivedita's international engagement is evident through her roles as a visiting fellow at institutions like Moscow State Institute for International Relations, Moscow State University, Institute for Oriental Studies in Russia, Institute for International Relations in Kiev, and the School of International Relations at Sichuan University, Center for Russia, East European and Eurasian studies, University of Texas and at St Edward University. She is a prolific author, having authored two books and edited seven others on subjects related to International Relations. Her research contributions encompass research papers, articles in various research journals, websites, newspapers, and chapters in edited books. Her insights frequently feature in international print and broadcast media. Dr. Nivedita has augmented her expertise through additional qualifications. She holds a qualification in women, borders, and migration studies from the University of Hannover, Germany, and another in Eurasian Studies from the Pushkin Institute, Russia.

Her research interests revolve around geopolitics, foreign policy, security's strategic dimensions, multilateral organizations, as well as, women and migration issues. Her remarkable achievements include being awarded the prestigious state award "Pushkin Medal" in 2013. She has also been the recipient of esteemed fellowships, including DAAD (Germany), RAS (Russia), CIMO (European Union), ICSSR (India), and ADA (Azerbaijan). Notably, Dr. Nivedita Kundu is a member of the Chemical Weapons Convention Coalition, actively working on weapons of mass destruction (WMD) issues and concerns. She is a regular speaker at CSP-OPCW (UN) sessions held at The Hague.

Dr. Nivedita Das Kundu has recently become an Advisor for the expert working committee of the Shanghai Cooperation Organization SCO-TEMP (Trade and Economic Multifunctional Platform for SCO countries). Presently she is also a non-residential fellow and life member at the prestigious institutions such as the United Services Institution of India, Science for Peace- at University of Toronto, and the Valdai Discussion Club of Russia.

Milton Keynes UK
Ingram Content Group UK Ltd.
UKHW010637240424
441619UK00001BA/131

9 788119 438952